Hindu

JOY OF LIFE

Hindu
JOY OF LIFE

Utpal K Banerjee

NIYOGI
BOOKS

Published by

NIYOGI
BOOKS

D-78, Okhla Industrial Area, Phase-I
New Delhi-110020, INDIA

Tel: 91-11-26816301, 26813350, 51, 52
Fax: 91-11-26813830

email: niyogibooks@gmail.com
Website: www.niyogibooks.com

Design: Arvind
ISBN: 978-81-89738-42-6

First Edition: 2006
This Edition: 2009

Printed at: Niyogi Offset Pvt. Ltd., New Delhi, India

To Shyamakanta and Nirupama,
my parents,
whose pious guidance
initiated me into
the Hindu world

Contents

Preface

Preface

The country was called Hindustan, a word that came from the mighty Hindu Kush Mountains on the northeast and had nothing to do with Hinduism. The term Hinduism was derived from 'Hindu', a name given by the visiting races and fighter hordes to the land and the people inhabiting the plains of the near-uncrossable River Indus. The land was, in reality, a continent: located within a cusp of high hills and raging seas; the people given to a natural penchant of absorption of all cultures, within their civilisation's ethos, without ever taking recourse to outbound physical conquests.

Sages of Hinduism, as it evolved without a revealed gospel, composed the hymns of Vedas – the world's first literature of awesome proportions – without vaunting iconic gods or temples. Hinduism, in myriad forms, manifestations and contents, grew to be a way of life, a celebration of the living beings: in wonder of nature, seeking the Supreme Being within and building customs, brick by brick, to regulate worldly behaviour through prayers and rituals. The Unmanifest was seen even in the soul of the lowly beggar. With the mutations that have gone through the ages, Hinduism continued to show a rare resilience to adopt and adjust, to argue on and then to assimilate ardent beliefs and utter nihilism. Countless viewpoints – and to cap it all – inherent and outside streams like Christianity, Buddhism, Jainism, Zoroastrianism, Islam and Sikhism all faired well alongside the majority community. Barring occasional aberrations, all of them have lived well in harmony. There was always space for everyone to flourish and remarkable tolerance that could not be matched in the annals of anti-Semiticism and anti-Islam crusades in this bloodletting planet.

Social intercourses and integrations have played a key role in binding communities together in a national mosaic of separate religious identities: favouring always a national identity. What gave Hinduism this resilience to accommodate, to live and let live, makes for a fascinating study: in order to look for the vitality that embraced one and all in the social discourses, arts and music, sports and countless joint festivals, in holding hands within the country and overseas. Those who went abroad left India, but India did not leave their hearts. This modest attempt is a quest for discovering that enduring vitality, *élan vital,* in the Hindu rubric. It is also an endeavour to demystify this fascinating religion from the dogmatic beliefs that may limit its understanding.

In preparing the revised edition, suggestions from Kamalini Dutt, Director of Archives (Doordarshan), have been most invaluable.

Utpal K Banerjee

Prologue: Élan Vital

Prologue: Élan Vital

Most Vedic gods were natural forces such as the sun, moon, fire or storm. One of the important indications of the gradual unification of India was the way the Vedic and non-Vedic myths and legends merged.

Nandi, the Bull, the mount for Shiva, worshipped at Chamundi Hill, Mysore.

Hinduism is not a religion that arose as a revelation (akin to Judaism) or was founded by an individual: held by believers as the Son of God (as in Christianity) or God's messenger (as in Islam). On the contrary, it is a philosophy, a way of life and its celebration. It has grown over much longer than three millennia and, although very much an ancient civilisation, has shown unabated vitality to continue in the contemporary era. This is what made Dr Heinrich Zimmer, the noted philosopher of the twentieth century, to observe:

> We of the Occident are about to arrive at a crossroads that was reached by the thinkers of India, some seven hundred years before Christ, to which the people of all civilisations come in the typical course of the development of their capacity and requirements for religious experience.

By seeking the roots of this vitality only, can one understand its need and relevance to the twenty-first century. Hinduism's basic beliefs and philosophy are not irrelevant to the problems of the modern world. In the past, these tenets influenced the thinking of nearly half of the world's population: partly through Hinduism itself, but also through its glorious offshoots, such as Jainism and Buddhism.

The Vedas, composed in the second millennium BC, provided a sense of awe and wonder at the mysteries of existence. According to Rabindranath Tagore, they bore a poetic statement of a people's collective reaction to the phenomenon of existence itself. It was the people's vigorous and uninhibited imagination: awakened at the dawn of civilisation to a sense of the inexhaustible mystique that is implicit in life. This led to speculation on theories of existence and life, as found in the Upanishads around the eighth century BC and in the later Hindu philosophy.

The other aspect is its moral code of behaviour. The conflict between what a man does and what a man ought to do is inherent in his concept of the nature of the universe. Recognising man as a creation of the Supreme and all men to be brothers, the Upanishads revealed their doctrine of the all-pervading God. The ideal of selfless work preached by the later Bhagavad Gita then became entirely relevant. The two main divisions of Hinduism have been the Vedic and the Brahmanical. The Vedic religion consisted of the worship – by performance of sacrifices in the open air, around a fire – of the elements and powers of nature, which had held the earliest humans in awe. Nature was clearly the main preoccupation, as most of the Vedic gods were natural forces like the sun, moon, fire, storm, and so on. One of the important indications of

Old illustrated manuscript from the Mahabharata.

the gradual unification of India was the way the Vedic and non-Vedic myths and legends merged together, giving rise to a common treasure-trove of mythology. But a common strand of moral and spiritual fibre ran through the immanent philosophy. There was a general recognition of the vastness of space and time, in which the earth was a mere speck of dust, life on it being transitory; hence triggering the need for noble pursuits.

The Brahmanical emphasis on rites and practices led to the emergence of anthropomorphic deities, with a strong urge to incorporate the non-Vedic tribes and other vocations *(bratya, anyavrata)* in the overall fold. Non-Vedic divinities (like the phallic symbol of *linga* for Creation) and the Brahmanical deities led to a remarkable assimilative process of animals – as mounts – like bull for Shiva,

In Vedic times, Nature worship was the essence of Hinduism.

peacock for Skanda (Kartikeya), lion for Durga, owl for Lakshmi, and swan for Saraswati, on a common platform for worship.

Alongside, deities like Brahma (for Creation), Vishnu (for Preservation) and Shiva (for Destruction) gradually replaced the Vedic worship of the wind (Pavana), rain (Varuna), thunder (Indra), sun (Sabita), moon (Chandrama), etc. Rituals and customs held the society together with a structured code of conduct for the purpose of noble living. While ceremonies for somber occasions and celebrations saw a man through life, ritual worship clearly addressed the divinity within.

Ideas and beliefs run through Hinduism like a thread providing it with the necessary psychological and intellectual staple. Much of the beliefs and practices emphasise that the order inherent in human life is essentially more secular than religious. It is these tenets that have provided the ongoing sustenance to the Hindu world.

The Upanishads centre around the doctrine of the Brahman (the all-pervading God) and the Atman (the self), pointing out that they both are the same. The Supreme has manifested Himself in every soul, as one is told dramatically in the Upanishads: *Tat Twam Asi* (Thou art That). This idea provides the core of most religious thoughts and was developed later by Samkara into his doctrine of Advaita (Non-duality). This is the monistic doctrine that denies the existence of the world as separate from that of God.

The Bhagavad Gita is different. Composed a few centuries after the Upanishads around 500 BC, it explores not the unreality of the world, but man's duties in it. It advocates the indestructibility of the soul, puts forward selfless action as an ideal and advises every human being about his or her duties. It is in this period – between 800 BC and 500 BC – that the main foundations of the modern Hinduism are laid. Polytheism gives way to monotheism, a moral code of conduct clearly emerges and the future trends of Hinduism are largely determined. As Jainism and Buddhism emerge, both develop the existing ideals of renunciation and love, and use the prevailing metaphysics of reincarnation, but with the emphasis qualitatively changed. After India has remained largely Buddhist for nearly half a millennium, Hinduism gains predominance once again. Buddhism, however, leaves behind considerable influence on Hinduism, adding to its mythology, expanding its cultural content and affecting its moral code.

Among the trends of post-Buddhist Hinduism, there is emphasis on three main ways of reaching God: *jnana* (knowledge), karma (action) and bhakti (devotion). While the Advaita Vedantists, for instance, emphasise the path of knowledge, many followers of the Bhakti movement take the path of exuberant devotion rather than practising calm meditation on the nature of God. Although bhakti is on the whole a non-Vedic tradition, it helps in

Lord Krishna steering towards the victory of the right over the wrong, explaining the sermons of the Bhagavad Gita to his disciple Arjun.

developing the idea of Avatara (Divine Incarnation), facilitating men to love a personal God rather than contemplate on the all-pervading, abstract Brahman of the Upanishads.

The Bhakti movement has often centred on avataras like Rama or Krishna. Even for devotion to non-incarnate gods, some form is attributed to the Formless for worship: as Vishnu or Shiva or Kali. The Bhakti movement flourished in the Middle Ages, reinforced by the Muslim Sufi tradition.

Besides religion, the cultural rubric of Hinduism has several aspects contributing to its vitality. Literature in Sanskrit is enormously rich in poetry, fiction, drama, ethics and literary criticism. The epics Ramayana and Mahabharata provide endemic fare in the near and distant lands of the South

Arati, a part of the evening ritual of worshipping deities, being performed at Har Ki Pohri, Haridwar.

and Southeast Asia. Even the scripts – Brahmi and Kharosthi – emerging at the turning of the millennium went to Tibet, Sri Lanka, Thailand on one side and to Afghanistan and Central Asia on

The incredibly detailed treatises on aesthetics and art – in profound harmony with iconography as well as religious scriptures – are a special contribution of Hindu culture. The articulation on *rasa* (emotion), felt by the *rasika* (audience) and evoked as an outcome of *bhava* (emotive expression by the artist-performer), is as detailed as are the cannons of architecture, sculpture, painting and poetry. There are very few civilisations in the world that have produced a masterly treatise like *Natya Shastra* – and its scores of commentaries over the centuries – which offer an integral vision of Indian visual and performing arts.

While rituals and ceremonies are for the god within, fairs and festivals are for the vox populi, where entire communities connect themselves with either Nature or manifest divinity, howsoever idealised and abstract. These occasions renew the social and psychic roots, and provide a fresh vitality to the community and individual life through an infectious brand of bonhomie and camaraderie. It is such vitality that has survived over aeons and sustained the inner spirit of overseas diaspora to scores of countries in recent centuries. The vitality of Hinduism has been endemic and contagious inspiring them to lead new life of prosperity, away from homeland, and yet retaining the cultural roots of their place of origin.

The following chapters are a brief account outlining the diverse vital forces, that is, élan vital, that have characterised this timeless civilisation and culture, and given it an unassailable grip to cope with the modernity of today.

the other. They also provide the staple to eleven scripts for the twenty-two highly developed Indian languages, besides many major dialects.

Chapter One
Noble Thoughts

Noble Thoughts

Indian thinkers looked up to the universe as a transitory entity, devoid of a beginning and end, and one that was not created at any specific time. Against an overwhelming vastness of the universe, Hindu philosophy dwelt upon the contrasting smallness of mankind.

In Hindu thought, the universe has no beginning; its vastness stands in stark contrast to the smallness of the earth as portrayed by the silhouette of temples against the horizon.

The Hindu philosophy, taken in the geographical sense of India, has had a synthetic outlook; where different problems of philosophy, ethics, logic, psychology and epistemology are paid due regard in the development of metaphysical thought. A striking breadth of outlook also prevails in the quest for truth, where a unique dialectic approach has been to ascertain, first, the prior view of the opponent by the proponent, followed by its refutation and then, the proof of the philosopher's own position, and finally, reaching the indisputable conclusion.

Though different schools of Indian philosophy present a diversity of views, we can discern in them the common stamp of an Indian culture, with a remarkable unity of moral and spiritual outlook. The main aim of *purushartha* (philosophical wisdom) is not the satisfaction of intellectual curiosity, but an enlightened life: led with farsight, foresight and insight. Every system, pro-Vedic or even anti-Vedic, has been moved by a spiritual disquiet at the evils

Sadhus proceed for a holy dip at Sangam, the confluence of the rivers Ganga, Yamuna and Saraswati, during Ardha Kumbha Mela, Allahabad.

affecting the world and a keenness to understand the source of these evils, the nature of the universe and the meaning of human life.

Yet a firm faith in an 'eternal moral order' has prevented the Indian mind from ending in despair and gloom, and dominated the entire history of

Indian philosophy, inspiring optimism and making man the master of his own destiny: by performing correct actions (karma) and reaping the benefits.

Indian thinkers have held the ignorance of reality as the cause of bondage (process of rebirths and consequent suffering) and liberation *(moksha)* from this process to be obtained by real knowledge of the world and the self, attainable even in this life. Continued meditation on truths, learnt through concentration and self-control (as in the Yoga System), is called for to remove deep-rooted false beliefs. Self-control, in fact, is needed to remove passions that obstruct good conduct. Belief in the potential of liberation has been common in all systems of philosophy.

The vastness of Space and Time became the underpinning of Indian thought and influenced its moral and metaphysical character. In contrast to the Western concept of a single-point-beginning of Time and Space, this was much more in keeping with the modern scientific conception of Time and Space as vast entities, as was in Einstein's space–time continuum. Similar ideas have appeared earlier in Indian literature, particularly the Puranic concept of the world that regions are separated from each other by millions of miles.

Indian thinkers looked up to the universe as devoid of any beginning *(anadi)* and not created at any particular time. With the overwhelming idea of the vast universe as its background, Indian thought naturally dwelt upon the extreme smallness of the earth, without a geocentric view, which is in consonance with modern science. The transitoriness

Hindu temples overlooking the ghats on the bank of River Ganga, Varanasi.

of earthly existence automatically led to the insignificance of earthly possessions. According to the Bhagavad Gita, while the human body is limited in Space and Time, the soul is eternal and human life is a rare opportunity. It can be utilised for attaining the immortal spirit and transcending the limitations of Space and Time.

Among the six major orthodox Hindu schools of philosophy (not rejecting Vedic authority), there are two schools directly based on Vedic texts—Mimamsa (emphasising the ritualistic aspects) and Vedanta (stressing on the speculative aspects); and four schools based on independent grounds—Samkhya, Nyaya, Vaisheshika and Yoga. The seventh heterodox Hindu school (rejecting Vedic authority) is the materialism of Charvaka, apart from the Buddhist and Jain schools of thought.

Mimamsa

Mimamsa considers the Vedas as eternal, self-existing, not the work of any person and, therefore, free from errors. Hence, the validity of the Vedic knowledge is self-evident. The Vedic commands to perform rituals are right (*dharma*) and what

The call of Nature: the Mimamsa School stresses on spiritual connectivity rather than rituals and rites.

they forbid is wrong *(adharma)*. Since the main objective of the Mimamsa School was to establish the authority of the Vedas, this school's most valuable contribution to Hinduism was its formulation of the rules of Vedic interpretation. Its adherents believed that any revelation must be proved by reasoning and should not be accepted blindly as dogma. In keeping with this belief, they laid great emphasis on *dharma*, which they understood as the performance of Vedic rituals. Mimamsa accepted the logical and philosophical teachings of other schools, but felt that these paid insufficient attention to right action. They believed that other schools of thought, who pursued *moksha* as their ultimate aim, were not completely free from desire and selfishness. According to Mimamsa, striving for liberation itself stemmed from a selfish desire to be free. Only by acting in accordance with the prescriptions of the Vedas could one attain salvation.

At a later stage, however, the Mimamsa School changed its views in this regard and began to teach the doctrines of God and *mukti* (freedom). Its adherents then advocated the release or escape of the soul from its constraints through what was known as *jnana* (enlightened activity). Though Mimamsa does not receive much scholarly attention these days, its influence can be felt in the life of the practising Hindu. All Hindu rituals, ceremonies and religious laws are influenced by it.

Vedanta

Arising out of the Upanishads, interpretations of Vedanta by Samkara and Ramanuja have had the most profound influence on Indian life. Samkara's teacher Gaudapada, a believer in strict monism,

Sunset in the woods. Vedantic thoughts consider the Self being continuous and inseparable from the Supreme.

asserted categorically that the external world was unreal; the only reality was the Brahman. Outer objects were purely subjective and the whole world was a vast illusion, like wakeful reams, there being nothing other than Brahman. Like the Buddhist spiritual absolutist Nagarjuna, Gaudapada denied even the possibility of change:

> There is no destruction, no creation, none in bondage, none endeavouring for release, none desirous of liberation, none liberated; this is the absolute truth.

Samkara's position was less extreme. While asserting the identity between the Brahman and Atman, and denying that the universe was outside

Last contemplation: identifying the Atman with the Brahman.

the pale of the Supreme, he observed that wakeful experiences were largely different from dreams and that external objects were not a mere form of personal consciousness.

In brief, the Vedanta emphasises that one supreme reality *(purusha)*, pervades the whole universe. All is God, the soul is God *(Ayam Atma Brahma)*; and there is no multiplicity here, in the infinite consciousness *(jnana)* and bliss *(ananda)*. Illusion *(maya)* is the nature of ignorance *(ajnanam)*. *Maya* as the power of God is no more different from God Himself than the burning power is from fire, leading to pure monism (Advaita). Vedanta, also known as the Uttara (later) Mimamsa School,

of Vedic religion that focussed on meditation, self-discipline and spiritual connectivity, rather than on more practical aspects of religion like rituals and rites.

The more abstruse Vedanta (meaning literally the end of the Vedas) is the essence of the Vedas, encapsulated in the Upanishads, which are commentaries on the four original books *(Rig, Yajur, Sama* and *Atharva)*. Vedantic thought drew on Vedic cosmology, hymns and philosophy. The most influential Vedantic thoughts, based on the Upanishads, consider the consciousness of the Self *(Jeevatman):* to be continuous with and indistinguishable from the consciousness of the Supreme or Brahman *(Paramatman)*.

Scholars and philosophers from both East and West, from Rabindranath Tagore, Mahatma Gandhi and Aurobindo Ghosh to Erwin Schrödinger, Henry David Thoreau and Ralph Waldo Emerson, acknowledge the Upanishads to be superlatively beautiful in poetry and rich in philosophy. But they do not form one single set of writings. There are over a hundred Upanishads and they do not form a unified system. While around thirteen or so Upanishads are accepted as the principal ones, a large number are extinct. They are traditionally grouped into twelve to thirteen primary Upanishads. The most notable, the largest and the first to be written down (approximately 1500 BC) is the *Brihadaranyaka Upanishad*.

Advaita, Dvaita and Vishistadvaita
Advaita is probably the best known of all Vedanta schools. Advaita literally means 'not two'. This is what we refer to as a monistic (or non-dualistic)

concentrates on the philosophical teachings of the Upanishads, rather than on the ritualistic injunctions of the Brahman. While the traditional Vedic Karma Kanda (the ritualistic components of religion) continued to be practised as meditative and propitiatory rites gearing society (through the Brahmins) to self-knowledge, more *jnana*-centred understanding began to emerge, as mystical streams

The emerging message: God is the Creator and is immanent in the universe.

system, which emphasises oneness. Its first great consolidator was Samkara (AD 788–820). Continuing the line of thought of some of the Upanishad teachers, Samkara expounded the doctrine of Advaita—a non-dualistic reality. By analysing the three states of experience (waking, dreaming and deep sleep), he exposed the relative nature of the world and established the supreme truth of the Advaita: the non-dual reality of Brahman in which Atman (the individual soul) and Brahman (the Ultimate Reality expressed in the Trimurti) are identified absolutely. Many see Adi Samkara drawing from the monist concepts what were visibly ingrained in formerly existing texts, those pre-dating the Buddha, like the more abstruse sections of the Vedas as well as the older Upanishads, several of which date as far back as 1000 BC, if not 1500 BC.

Subsequent Vedantists debated whether the reality of Brahman was *saguna* (with attributes) or *nirguna* (without attributes). Belief in the concept of *saguna* Brahman gave rise to a proliferation of devotional attitudes and more widespread worship of Vishnu and Shiva. Advaita Vedanta is strictly grounded in a belief that the ultimate truth is *nirguna* Brahman. The Vishistadvaita and Dvaita schools believed in an ultimately *saguna* Brahman. Ramanuja (AD 1040–1137) was the foremost proponent of the concept of Sriman Narayana as the supreme Brahman. He taught that the Ultimate Reality had three aspects: *Ishvara* (Vishnu), *chit* (soul) and *achit* (matter). Vishnu is the only independent reality, while soul and matter are dependent on God for their existence. Because of this qualification of the Ultimate Reality, Ramanuja's system is known as Vishistadvaita (Qualified Non-dualism). This was expanded by Purnaprajna Anandatirtha Madhva (AD 1238–1317) who identified God with Vishnu, but his view of reality was purely dualistic and is, therefore, called Dvaita (dualistic). There was also another school, which endeavoured to combine both Dvaita

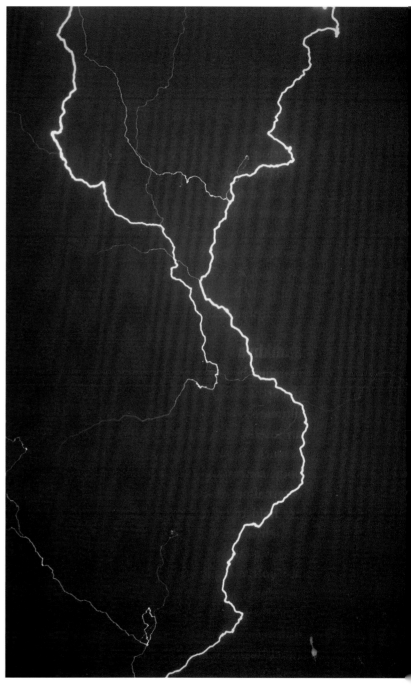

Descent of enlightenment: the distinction of the self and intellect.

33

and Advaita in a single tenet of Dvaita–Advaita, but with relatively little success.

One endearing and comprehensive way to explain the three abstract principles is to use the epigrammatic expression: *rasyate* (God has created as well as permeated His creation); *rasayate* (God has created, but has kept Himself aloof from his creation); and both *rasyate* and *rasayate* (God is both the creator of the universe and also immanent in His creation). Chaitanya (AD 1486–1534), a devotee of Krishna, proposed a synthesis between the monist and dualist philosophies by stating that the soul is equally distinct *(bheda)* and non-distinct *(abheda)* from God, whom he identified as Krishna, and that this, although unthinkable *(achintya),* is experienced in devotion.

Samkhya

Founded by Sage Kapila, Samkhya is the oldest of the orthodox philosophical systems, admitting two ultimate realities: *purusha* and *prakriti. Purusha* is an intelligent principle and consciousness is its essence. The inner self is quite distinct from the body, senses and mind. In contrast, *prakriti* is an external unconscious principle whose constituents are held together in equilibrium. An important Samkhya contribution is the doctrine of *Triguna* (three qualities or dispositions of Nature). These are: *sattva* (light, purity, harmonious existence), *rajas* (energy, passion) and *tamas* (inertia, dullness). Together, they define steadiness, activity and dullness. When the equilibrium of the *gunas* (qualities) is disturbed, the world order evolves from this disturbance, due to the proximity of *purusha* and *prakriti. Kaivalya* (liberation) consists of the realisation of the difference between the two. It is made evident that the evolution of the world has its starting point in the association of *purusha* with *prakriti,* representing the awakening of nature and appearance of creative thought.

In a sense, this is a dualistic philosophy, but there are differences between the Samkhya and Western forms of dualism. In the West, the fundamental distinction is between mind and body. In Samkhya, however, it is the duality between the self *(purusha)* and matter, and the latter incorporates what Westerners would normally refer to as 'mind'. The self tends to confuse itself with *buddhi* (intellect), but when the knowledge of this distinction is achieved, *prakriti* no longer bonds the soul. The person (soul) becomes a disinterested spectator of worldly happenings. At death, the bonding between *purusha* and *prakriti* is completely snapped – making the emancipated soul, unlike other souls – free from rebirth. Bondage, according to this philosophy, is due to ignorance, and emancipation comes through knowledge.

Samkhya has been described as an atheistic philosophy, since the *Samkhya Prabachana Sutra* (attributed to Sage Kapila) finds it unnecessary to make any assumption about the existence of God, and it does not deny God either, remarkably akin to much of Buddhist philosophy. It maintains that the existence of God cannot be proved by evidence, but the later Samkhya philosophers like Vijnana Bhikshu abandoned this agnostic position.

Nyaya

Propounded by Aksapada Gautama (300 BC), it is a realistic philosophy, based mainly on logical grounds.

Like Samkhya, it too admits of sources of knowledge as perception, inference, comparison and testimony. The objects of knowledge are: the self; body; senses and their objects; cognition; mind; activity; mental defects; rebirth; feelings of pleasure and pain; suffering; and freedom from suffering.

It accepts that God created this world out of eternal atoms, space, time, ether, mind and soul, that individual souls *(jiva)* might enjoy pleasure or suffer pain, according to their actions. The Nyaya School of philosophical speculation is based on a text called the *Nyaya Sutra*. The most important contribution made by this school is its methodology, based on a system of logic that has subsequently been adopted by most other Indian schools (orthodox or not), much in the same way

Meditation in solitude. Yoga emphasises on meditating on the Ishvara.

that Western science and philosophy can be said to be largely based on Aristotelian logic.

Nyaya is not merely logic for its own sake. Its followers believed that obtaining valid knowledge was the only way to obtain release from suffering. They, therefore, took great pains to identify valid sources of knowledge and to distinguish these

Sculptured manifestation of Shiva in the Tanjavur Temple.

from mere false opinions. According to the Nyaya School, there are four sources of knowledge or *pramanas*: perception, inference, comparison and testimony. Knowledge obtained through each of these can be either valid or invalid, and the Nyaya scholars identified in each case what it took to make knowledge valid, and in the process, came up with several explanatory schemes. In this sense, Nyaya is probably the closest Indian equivalent to contemporary Western analytical philosophy.

An important later development in Nyaya is the system of *Navya Nyaya* (New Logic), founded by Gangesha (AD 1200). His *Tattva Chudamani*, the standard text in the new school, built up a more rigorous structure for this discipline: to deal with the knowledge of the external world.

Vaisheshika

Allied to Nyaya, Vaisheshika aims at the liberation of the individual self, classifying all objects of knowledge as: substance, quality, action, generality, particularity, relation of inheritance and non-existence. Regarding acceptance of personal God and liberation of the individual soul, it is substantially the same as Nyaya.

Founded by Kanada (300 BC), his *Vaisheshika Sutra* postulates an atomic pluralism. In terms of this school of thought, all objects in the physical universe are reducible to nine substances: atoms (four kinds), space, time, ether, mind and soul. All the nine substances existed before the world was formed and God only fashioned them into an orderly universe. God is thus the creator of the world, but not its constituents. Thus, the Vaisheshika philosophy, while not atheistic, is different from most schools of traditional Hindu theology. In fact, there were so many unorthodox thinkers in this school that Samkara, the great champion of Vedanta, described the followers of Vaisheshika as *Ardha-Vainashika*s (Half-Nihilists)!

In its classical form, the Vaisheshika School differed from the Nyaya School in one crucial respect—while the latter accepted four sources of valid knowledge, the former accepted only perception and inference.

The evolution of these two systems, however, has been closely linked with each other throughout history. Together, these systems represent the relatively analytical branch of Hindu philosophy.

Contemplation at the day's end.

Yoga

The philosophical basis of Yoga is the same as that of Samkhya, *i.e.,* accepting knowledge. But unlike Samkhya, it also admits of the existence of a personal God who controls the process of evolution and is, as one might expect, omniscient and omnipotent. Periodically, He dissolves the cosmos to initiate the process of evolution again. As a practice, to attain liberation, Yoga recognises five levels of mental functions, namely, the totally dissipated condition; somewhat subdued softened condition; fully pacified condition; state of concentration; and cessation of contemplation.

The last two levels of the mind are conducive to total Yogic concentration for which eight practices are performed—restraint, moral culture, posture, breath control, withdrawal of senses, attention, meditation and total concentration. Various methods of concentration as well as methods of suppressing those mental activities that increase our bondage are recommended: by making us more dependent on *prakriti*. The Yoga system of exercises is still commonly practised in India on a psychosomatic basis. Apart from those seeking emancipation, there are those who find Yoga to be a useful way of keeping the mind and body healthy. There are also those from the West, who have been attracted by its promise of prompt development of supernatural power: a promise that seems to have appealed at all times of history!

The Yoga philosophy is considered to have risen from the Samkhya system. Its primary text is the Bhagavad Gita, which explores the four primary systems: karma, jnana, bhakti and raja. Sage Patanjali wrote *Yoga Sutra*, an influential text on Raja Yoga. The significant difference between the Samkhya and the Yoga schools is that the latter not only incorporates the concept of *Ishvara* into its metaphysical worldview, which the former does not, but it also upholds *Ishvara* as the ideal upon which to meditate. This is because *Ishvara* is the only aspect of *purusha* that has not become entangled with *prakriti*. It also refers to the Brahman/Atman terminology and concepts that are found in the Upanishads, thus breaking from the Samkhya School by adopting Vedantic monist concepts.

The Yoga System prescribes for the gradual attainment of physical and mental control as well as mastery over one's body, mind and self, until one's consciousness has intensified sufficiently to acquire the awareness of one's real Self (the soul, or Atman, as distinct from one's feelings, thoughts and actions). Realisation of the goal of Yoga is known as *moksha*, *nirvana* and *samadhi*. They all speak to the realisation of the Atman as being nothing other than the Infinite Brahman.

Charvaka

Interestingly, although accepted within the fold of Hindu metaphysical thoughts, Charvaka's philosophy is out-and-out an atheist one. Based on the tenets of pure materialism, Sage Charvaka held direct perception as the only valid source of real knowledge.

All indirect sources of knowledge like inference, testimony of other persons, etc., are unreliable and can prove misleading. The materials comprise earth *(kshiti)*, water *(ap)*, fire *(tej)* and air *(marut)*, all of whose existence are directly known through the senses.

Above all, survival of man in any form after death is unproved and existence of God – who cannot be perceived – is a myth. The world is not made by God, but by the automatic combination of material elements. The highest end of life for a rational man is enjoyment of the greatest amount of pleasure in this life alone.

Basically, the cultural evolution of India that took place around the seventh century BC was full of heterodox creeds and opinions. Charvaka was the best-known teacher of the Lokayata School of thought, which considered physical sensory data to be the only source of knowledge and challenged the whole edifice of Hindu metaphysics. This school was prevalent in pre-Buddhist times and undoubtedly had numerous adherents from that period onwards to the present day. The Lokayata School allowed only perception as a means of knowledge and rejected inference. It recognised as the sole reality the elements of matter and taught that when a body is formed by the combination of elements, the spirit also comes into existence, just like the intoxicating quality generated with the mixture of special materials. With the destruction of the body, the spirit returns again to nothingness.

The above resonates well with one of the oft-quoted aphorisms of Charvaka: 'Live well even by borrowing, for, once cremated, there is no return!' This rejection of after-life and reincarnation is also echoed in a passage of the epic Ramayana, where Javali, a Brahmin, advises the superhero Rama against giving up his kingdom, saying:

> I grieve for those who, abandoning the pleasures
> of the world, seek to acquire merit for felicity
> hereafter and sink to an untimely death; I do not grieve for others. Men waste food and other precious things by offering them as sacrifices in honour of their departed ancestors. O Rama, has a dead man ever partaken of food? ... O Ramachandra, these scriptural instructions were laid down by learned men, skilled in inducing others to give, and finding other means of obtaining wealth, thus subjugating the simple-minded. ... O Rama, be wise, there exists no world but this, that is certain! Enjoy that which is present and cast behind that which is unpleasant!

The utter catholicity of Hindu philosophy is proven by its embracing a widely divergent range of philosophy, including all shades of agnosticism like that of Javali, and even the utterly atheist views of Charvaka! It is this diversity that lends Hinduism its special place in the world.

Chapter Two

Worship

Worship

Brahman and Atman are the underpinning principles permeating the universe. The Upanishads identified Brahman with the primeval anthropomorphic being, purusha, who is manifested in Lord Brahma, the Creator of the Universe.

A temple priest performing puja.

In their deep quest of life's mystery and meaning, Vedic sages realised an eternal truth which they named Brahman and Atman, the impersonal principles that permeated the universe. The scholastic pursuit for knowledge of Brahman and Atman was, later, the staple of several Upanishads. Knowledge of the Brahman's self, for instance, was Truth, Wisdom and Eternity according to *Taittiriya Upanishad* and knowledge of Atman's self was endurance, purity, enlightenment and freedom, as per Samkara's annotation of the Bhagavad Gita. In finality, Brahman and Atman were one and the same, to the wise and the contemplative.

The manifestations of the highest spiritual reality have been eulogised in the *Rig Veda* where the elemental forces of nature found mention. The Vedic religion indeed is quite 'of earth, earthy'. While the *Rig Veda* contains prayers, the *Sama Veda* constitutes hymns, the *Yajur Veda* emphasises on the sacrificial fire and the *Atharva Veda* highlights magical rites, beliefs and cults.

The Brahman – neuter in gender and with no distinguishing characteristics perceptible to the five senses – came to be identified in the Upanishads with the primeval anthropomorphic being *purusha* from whom the universe originated, as described in the *Rig Veda*. The manifestation led to the male god Brahma, as the universal creator, preserver and destroyer in early epic mythology. Brahma was the self-existent *(svayambhu)* primal god and the ancient 'grandfather' *(pitamaha)*, as reflected in composite sculptures. Saraswati, seen as the 'active power' of Brahma, has survived in the modern Hindu world as a more important figure than Brahma himself and is the divinity for education.

Vedic Deities

They were the deified natural forces, evolving out of the fear and wonderment of the thinking man while facing the unknown elements, and revealing three principal characteristics. First, Agni, as the principal deity, and most hymns were addressed to him: as the sun in the sky, lightning in the air and fire on earth, thus covering all three spaces. Second, all deities were the children of Prajapati Brahma, to whom the *asuras* (demons) and mortals were siblings, thus visualising a primeval egalitarian state, from which hierarchy had evolved. Third, there were no anthropomorphic gods and their temples, as no images were made of the deities and no temples

Agni worshipped as the messenger between mankind and the deities.

created as their abode; only their qualities and attributes were annotated in human terms.

Revered as the mediator between men and deities, Agni was the protector of human homes and was honoured for his role in *yajna* (sacrificial fire). All oblations to the sacred fire were made in the name of his consort *Swaha* and considered essential to all religious rites. *Dyaus* (heaven) and *prithvi* (earth) were other ancient deities, spoken of in the *Rig Veda* as 'great, wise, energetic', who 'promoted righteousness and bestowed benefits upon their followers'. Indra, once the most popular deity of the firmament, was deemed armed with *vajra* (thunderbolt). Presiding over *Indralok* (the celestial court), his courtiers included *apsara*s (divine dancers), *gandharva*s (musicians) and *kinnara*s (performers): an early affirmation of performing arts in the celestial scheme of things!

The forty-nine *maruta*s were the assistant deities to Indra: who harnessed fierce storms in the monsoon skies to defeat their foe *vritra* (droughts), hence keeping with the unfavourable climate encountered during the Aryan progress to the east and south. Varuna was the deity of the vast oceans, to whom many beautiful prayers were offered. Parjanya was there to control rains and nourish plants and living creatures, while Pushan was to 'drive away the way-layer, thief and robber', as per the *Rig Veda*. Soma was the deity of *Somrasa,* the celestial intoxicant!

Surya was the most important life-giver, to whom the most sacred *Gayatri Mantra* was addressed. One needed to craft this world and hence Vishwakarma

Lord Shiva, the source of all knowledge, at Omkareshwar, Madhya Pradesh.

was the architect and workman of the deities. Usha was the most poetically described young Goddess of Light in Vedic hymns. Pawana (Vayu) was the Deity of Winds with Indra, and Yama was the Deity of Death and Righteousness who protected the good and the pious.

Puranic Gods

Gradually, the anthropomorphic gods (residing in the sanctum sanctorum of their temples) emerged in the Puranic period of the early Christian millennium and Hinduism reached its pinnacle when Brahma, the Creator, came to be seen as one of the *Trimurti* (Triad of Gods), the other two being Vishnu, the Preserver and Shiva, the Destroyer. They together represented three forms of the unmanifested Supreme Being. Vishnu was often seen as the divine essence of the gods, and the *Rig Veda* had extolled his three cosmic strides: referring to the evolution of life from the physical to the ethereal. Vishnu, identified as Narayana of the self-existent source, rose to prominence in the Brahmans (ritual commentaries composed by the priests of the Vedic sacrifices). Shiva, on the other hand, evolved from the Vedic deity Rudra presiding over storm, disease and death.

The decline of Indra, the leader of the Vedic deities, took place late in the pre-Christian era, by which time, Rudra emerged as Shiva in association with the *linga,* the phallic symbol taken from the non-Vedic phallus worshippers. Shiva, first portrayed as an ascetic, was also named Pashupati (Master of Beasts), in the epic literature. In the

Devi Durga, Mother-Goddess manifesting female energy.

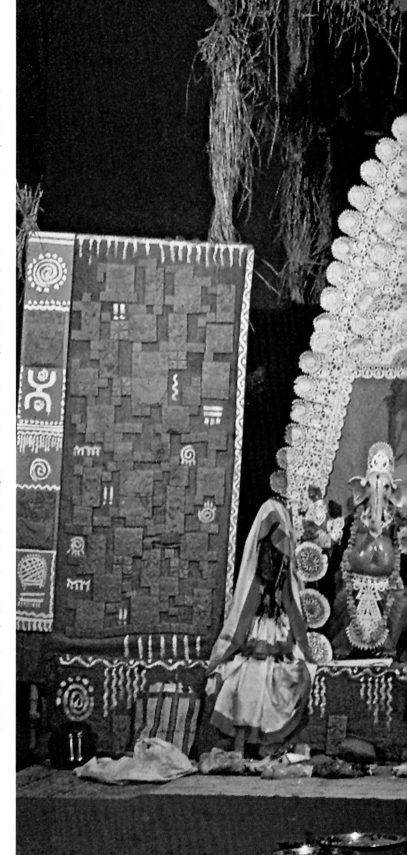

South, the icon of Dakshinamurti expressed the same vision of Shiva as the source of all sacred knowledge; the idol of Nataraja portrayed him as the Lord of Dance; and that of the androgynous Ardhanarishwara projected him as a superb symbol uniting the male and female aspects. By then, the other Vedic deities of the elemental forces like

Devi Saraswati, the Goddess of Knowledge, Music and Art, and the consort of Brahma.

Varuna, Pawana, Agni, Kubera (Protector of Wealth) and the Ashwini Kumars (Dispenser of Medicine) etc., were generally no longer worshipped.

Kartikeya (Skanda), the God of War, is especially worshipped in the South, as the son of Shiva and Parvati. While Shiva's bull, Nandi, is one of the most widespread sacred symbols of the ancient world, Hanumana is a denizen of forests who, as the faithful follower of Rama, is worshipped all over the West and the North.

Devi

Although the Vedas had extolled the virtues of predominantly male deities, Hindu tradition recognises Devi (Shakti) as the Mother-Goddess of the pre-Vedic times who came into prominence in the Puranic period as the slayer of the buffalo-demon Mahishasura after wielding the masculine powers of all the gods who had failed to vanquish him. The goddesses of the Vedic tribes took on the role of intermediaries between man and the gods, and the *Mundaka Upanishad* described the Vedic rituals through which the goddesses were instrumental for human access to the heavenly world. Uma Haimavati (same as Parvati) is described in the *Kena Upanishad* as the Daughter of the Snow Mountains who became the consort of Shiva.

Similarly worshipped is Lakshmi, the consort of Vishnu, who is also considered to be the Goddess of Wealth. The devotional tradition of Tantras of the late first millennium AD elevated the female principle above the dominance of masculine deities and the Mother-Goddess was, like the concept of Brahman, beyond tangible manifestation. 'She who remains, pervading the entire world, entirely in the

Ganesha symbolises good fortune and is the most auspicious deity, worshipped at the beginning of any new task.

form of intelligent thought' is how the *Markandeya Purana* regarded her.

Devi, as the supreme feminine spirit, came to be known as *swarupa:* not as incarnation on earth but as the symbol of the total energy of all gods. If one counts the *bhayankari* (destructive) manifestations of Devi, they are found in the eleventh–twelfth-century *Devi-Bhagavata Purana* as Maha Kali, Maha Lakshmi and Maha Saraswati. Amongst these manifestations of Devi, the most extolled in visual and performing arts is Devi as Durga.

In eastern India, the worship of Durga assumes a familial form, with Ganesha from the west, Kartikeya and Saraswati from the south and Lakshmi from the north, it is seen as a unique reflection of Indian unity. There are accompanying fauna as the divine mounts, mouse (for Ganesha), peacock (for Kartikeya), swan (for Saraswati), owl (for Lakshmi) and lion (for Durga), perhaps mirroring an early Aryan-Dravidian convergence of respective totems.

The *bhayankari* manifestations are—Lalita (both *bhayankari* and *shubhankari* who fought the greedy demon Bhandasura); Chamunda (who killed the lascivious demons Shumbha and Nishumbha); Chandi (who helped to eliminate the demons Madhu and Kaitabha, born out of the ear-wax of Vishnu, by waking up the latter from illusory sleep); and Kalika (who licked out every drop of blood from the mutilated demon Raktabeeja who would otherwise proliferate in the world). These myths, often varied, have deep shades of meaning, to conjure Devi's fight against base animal instincts, such as avarice for wealth; lust for women; and power leading to corruption. Most of these instincts are inside all of us, only to be curbed and controlled, for which ovations are sung. The remarkable underpinning is the creation of a balance between good and evil, and restoring stability by not eliminating the latter (which will be unrealistic), but overpowering it with good.

In the *shubhankari* (ameliorative) manifestations of Devi, one can count a group of *Sapta Matrikas* (Seven Mothers)—Brahmansi (Shakti of Brahma); Maheshwari (Shakti of Shiva); Kaumari (Shakti of Skanda); Vaishnavi (Shakti of Vishnu) Varahi (Shakti of Varaha-Vishnu); Indrani (Shakti of Indra) and Chamunda (an aspect of Devi herself). In contrast, the *Dasa Maha Vidyas* (Ten Great Manifestations of Durga) range over both the benevolent and malevolent forces—Kali, Tara, Shodashi, Bhuvaneshwari, Vairabi, Chhinnamasta, Dhumavati, Bagala, Matangi and Kamala.

The male-female complimentarity is articulated through the Ardhanarishwara icons, the androgynous forms of Shiva and Parvati. The associated myths also establish the cardinal principle of harmony—Shiva's creation of aberrations is to establish accessibility to prayers (expounded in many legends) and Shakti's destruction of aberrations is to subdue the evil and the malevolent, and restore balance.

Ganesha

As one of the most popular Hindu gods, Ganesha has his image revered across India and indeed in the entire East and Southeast Asia, and even amongst Buddhists and Jains. This elephant-headed and pot-bellied god is the most auspicious one for offering prayers before undertaking any new task. Of the legions of gods and goddesses whose images adorn the walls of temples, shops and homes, Ganesha is the easiest to recognise: the one with the elephant head.

In one hand, he holds a *parasu* (hatchet), which symbolises the cutting away of vanity and false teachings. In another hand, he holds an *ankusha* (goad), symbolising the logic that cuts through illusion. In the third hand is a *pasa* (noose), representing the restraint of passions and desires. Sometimes, one hand also gestures fearlessness and reassurance. The fourth hand holds a *modaka* (sweet), epitomising the universe: where the outward worldliness has no worth, but within is the bliss. His extended stomach has a Tantric

Rock-cut sculpture of Shiva-Parvati along with Ganesha in Ravana Padi cave, Karnataka.

interpretation of Kundalini reaching Muladhara and the feeling of satiation ebbing away.

Trinity—Brahma–Vishnu–Maheshwara

Brahma, the Creator, is said to have sprung from a lotus in the primeval waters out of Vishnu's navel, symbolising rebirth from the seed of past manifestations that have been preserved in Vishnu. The origin of the Vedas is attributed to Brahma. He is also intimately connected with the arts, as architecture, painting, dance, music and drama are seen as efforts to bring glimpses of the divine to earth. In order to give an understanding of the real nature of joy, Brahma is said to have written the

Rock formations sanctified as pindies *outside the Vaishno Devi cave. They represent three goddesses: Kali, Lakshmi and Saraswati.*

Natya Veda, as the fifth Veda, by culling out concepts from the *Rig Veda;* music from the *Sama Veda;* words and mime from the *Yajur Veda;* and *rasa* from the *Atharva Veda.*

In the Triad, Vishnu is believed to be the combination of three icons: Vasudeva-Krishna (the Man-God), the Vedic god and Narayana (the Cosmic God). Identified as the sun in the four Vedas, the qualities and attributes representing Vishnu's manifestations are symbolised in his numerous images and depicted in three attitudes: *shayana-murti* (as sleeping above the primordial ocean); *sthanaka-murti* (standing up with four arms); and *asana-murti* (sitting). The four arms of Vishnu symbolise: four stages of life, four goals for living (righteousness, wealth, pleasure and liberation); four cardinal directions; four castes; and four *yugas* (ages). He holds in his four hands four objects: *sudarshana chakra* (discus) symbolising mental power; *sharanga* (bow) denoting destructive aspect; *shankha* (conch) indicating primeval sound; and *kaumodaki gada* (mace) representing power of knowledge.

The Bhagavata movement centred round the adoration of Vishnu, as first seen in the Tusam rock inscription of fourth–fifth century. Till the early Guptas, incarnations of Vishnu were variously mentioned in the *Satapatha-Brahmansa, Taittairiya-Samhita,* Mahabharata and Puranas. Around the ninth century, Srimad Bhagavata enumerated the *Dasavataras* (ten incarnations) as: Matsya (fish), Kurma (tortoise), Varaha (boar), Narasimha (the man-lion), Vamana (the dwarf), Parasurama (the angry Brahmin), Rama (the perfect human), Balarama (the agricultural hero), the Buddha and Kalki (the redeemer of righteousness, who is yet to appear). Celebrated in all visual and performing arts, *Dasavatara Stotra* of Jayadeva (twelfth century) followed the Bhagavata and was included in Adi Guru Granth by Guru Arjun Singh. In this presentation, Krishna was taken as the original form of Vishnu and Buddhism was seen as akin to the reformation movement of Martin Luther in Christianity.

Rudra of the Vedas is described as Maheshwara Shiva in the *Ashtadhyayi* grammar by Panini in the sixth century BC, in *Arthashastra* by Kautilya in the third century BC and in *Grihya Sutra* by Samkara in the eighth century AD. Rudra-Shiva, as a benevolent god, is eulogised in the epics and the Puranas. The human representation in Uma-Maheshwara and Ardhanarishwara forms occur since the Kushana times, with Nandi joining in as part of the family.

The post-Gupta era brought in new images of Shiva, such as Lingodbhava Yoga-Dakshina, Vinadhara, Samhara and Bhairavamurti. The *Agama* treatises mention that *linga*s may be *svayambhu* (always existent) or man-made. The five main aspects of the Shiva-sculpted manifestations are: Vamadeva, Tatpurusha, Aghora, Sadyojata and Ishana.

Among the anthropomorphic representations, the Urdhareta images have been carved artistically from the Kushana period onwards. Shiva, as a

Krishna, the manifestation of Vishnu on earth, is usually depicted as a young man standing with one leg bent in front of the other and playing the flute.

master of yoga, music and other arts, is known as Dakshinamurti.

Vishnu's ten incarnations on earth were visualised as necessary to rescue truth and goodness from the clutches of evil. They almost

Most Hindu deities are worshipped as personifications of natural forces or abstract concepts. River Ganga, the holiest river in Hindu mythology is worshipped as Ganga Devi in Haridwar.

encapsulate the evolutionary process of mankind. The reincarnation of Vishnu signifies that all forms of life are related. The role of the animal in Indian myth and religion is a pointer to this aspect, since the divinity and animal world are never seen as opposed to each other, but as points on a continuum. Animals are worshipped, whether as mounts of deities, like the bull of Shiva, or as their representatives, like the cat associated with Shashti, the Goddess of Childbirth. Shiva's massive causal strength is conveyed by his mount: the noble, snow-white bull.

Durga confronts the dark forces in battle, as well as astrides a lion or a tiger (as Vaishno Devi depicts), creatures of grace and ferocity. The wise, elephant-headed Ganesha has as his mount the modest mouse, which patiently overcomes great obstacles. It is to be remembered that the worship of Ganesha is symbolic of primordial power and spiritual equilibrium and, as such, is a starting point of human civilisation.

Krishna

Widely worshipped as god and yet intensely human in daily living, Krishna is one of the major sources of guidance for Hindus. He is taken as a complete manifestation of Vishnu on earth. The Bhagavad Gita, as narrated by Krishna to Arjuna before the great battle in Mahabharata, is considered to be an epitome of wisdom. It provides three practical ways of reaching the supreme ideal: *jnana* (way of knowledge), karma (way of action) and bhakti (way of devotion). There is no prescribed form of service to the Lord and the devotee is open to assume any state like: *Dasya,* taking Krishna to be the master and the devotee a servant, as did the blind poet Surdas; *Sakhya,* in which Krishna is a friend or colleague, as was Sudama or Arjuna or Draupadi; *Vatsalya,* in which the devotee sees Krishna as a child and herself as a parent, as did Yashoda and as does every Indian mother (viewing the child as Bala Gopala, the little Krishna!); and *Madhurya* (or *Shringara*), in which the worshipper sees Krishna as a lover, as did Radha and the *gopis.*

The Krishna mythology encompasses a myriad *lilas* (playlets), broadly falling into four categories. First, the childhood pranks of Krishna establish the divine *maya* of the Supreme, while the child remains as lovable as ever. Second, Krishna foils all attempts made by demons to kill him. These acts, interestingly, do not quell evil permanently (which is impossible in the real world), but purifying them by the Lord's touch, leading to redemption. The third is to establish the undoubted competitive edge that Krishna has over other godheads in their hierarchy. The fourth, and the most charming *lila* is the mosaic of music and dance of Krishna with the *gopis* as a group and his *amour propre* Radha in particular. The last *lila* makes him not only hugely accessible to every man's fantasy, but also provides a romantic outlet to the collective imagination.

Lesser Deities

In a highly ingenious inversion of roles, mortals could also attain godhood through extremely pious deeds, and become ascetics to whom the gods revealed knowledge. As sanctified by the *Vishnu Purana,* when Brahma wished to populate the world, he created mind-born sons, like himself, who are visible in the night sky as *Saptarshi Mandala* (constellation of the Great Bear). They are: Angiras, the *Rig Veda* priest who is said to have 'drawn forth fire' for the use of men; Atri, the author of great many Vedic hymns; Bhrigu, one of the progenitors of men to whom Manu's institute of Hindu law was confided; Daksha, 'able, competent and intelligent', the father of the stars; Kratu, creator of several *valakhilyas* (pigmy sages); Marichi, chief of the sixty *marutas*; and Vasistha, 'most wealthy', celebrated Vedic sage, author of several Vedic hymns.

What is remarkable in the multiplicity of Hindu divinity is, first, their logical evolution; second, that they embrace a fascinating range of symbolism; and, third, they accommodate vastly different convictions and widely divergent customs in a large and diverse country with many distinct pursuits. But what is even more striking is the personification of abstract concepts in the form of divinities, such as Goddess Sarawati, who is seen not as a young lady sitting on a white swan with a *vina* in hand, but as an embodiment of knowledge and arts.

The quality of imagination is the same that would be needed, say, to appreciate the poetry of Kalidasa's *Meghaduta* (the Cloud Messenger), in which a forlorn lover, in exile, urges the fleeting cloud to carry his message of desperate longing to his lover, living far away. A great part of the Hindu religious practice involves appealing to the human imagination. In the *Isa Upanishad,* even God is described as a *kavi* (seer), a term that later came to mean a poet!

Chapter Three
Noble Living

Noble Living

Hinduism is an agglomeration of many cultures. This is probably most clearly visible in the multiple patterns of social norms and customs. Every kind of religious act is represented by a corresponding Hindu ritual.

Prayers offered by repeating mantras glorifying the deity.

Dharma (religion) is a code of conduct supported by the general conscience of the people. It is not subjective in the sense that the conscience of the individual imposed, nor external in the sense that the law enforces it. Dharma does not force men into virtue, but trains them for it. It is not a fixed code of mechanical rules, but a living spirit, which grows and moves in response to the development of the society. Further, the conscience of the individual requires a guide and he has to be taught to realise his purpose and live according to spirit and not sense.

– Dr S. Radhakrishnan

Hinduism has been a product of many cultures. This is probably most clearly visible in the multiple patterns of social mores and customs. Every kind of religious act, beginning from the sacrifices of the Vedic Aryans to the rituals of primitive animistic practices, can be seen in the body of Hindu rituals. While the meaning of most of these customs has changed over time and many of them are now purely symbolical, they still form a significant part of the Hindu way of life.

For the purpose of noble living, the highly developed rituals are a code of rules by which the Shakti (power) essential to the winning of *punya* (virtue) can be preserved and enhanced and *papa* (vice) can be avoided. The merit of virtue is related to *dharma* to living in the society and to appropriate behaviour that changes according to time, place and person, the reverse of which is demerit or vice.

On the rules regarding cleanliness, chastity to purify the mind is essential before a sacrifice or before undertaking a *vrata* (vow). Ideas associated with charity show how both merits and demerits

Devotees performing rituals at the bank of the holy Ganga.

Offering salutations.

God Savita's effulgent brilliance, may he guide us in our devotions.'

Spiritual Rituals

The central unifying feature of all Indian spiritual life is *kriya* (action): the timely fulfilment of ritual performance. It is according to the principles of right action that life runs its course. Rituals assert the Indian sense of human community and of collaboration with the creative rhythms of the world. The history of Indian rituals commenced with the Vedic period around 1500 BC. The Vedic tradition of *Yajna* began with the establishment of the centre; the orientation of sacred space; the laying of the brick for the fire altar; the kindling of the sacred fire; the timing of the rites; and the pouring of the libation, with all the ceremonies having their source in the world's oldest literature: the *Rig Veda*.

Rituals (and the associated mythology that gave them their numerous dimensions of meaning) were amplified at the period of the Brahmanas during 900–700 BC. There were texts in which various groups of sages provided commentaries on the Vedic hymns, describing the sacrificial ceremonies and recording the histories and significances of the ritual observances. In the post-Vedic period, reform movements emerged, advocating the ascetic path to personal liberation. Alongside these movements were the texts of the *Shada Darshana* (six schools) of Hindu philosophy, described earlier. Out of them, Mimamsa, while directing attention to Vedic thought, reformulated the meaning of the fundamental fire sacrifice in metaphysical terms.

The Grihya Sutras and the Samhitas (ritual handbooks) were the earliest texts concerned with

are related to power through the give-and-take of gift, as giving a gift is meant to ennoble the giver. Old age is venerated, providing spontaneous respect to the elder and thus keeping family ties intact. Similarly, honorifics of royalty or divinity given to the bridal pair are aimed at enhancing the divinity of the nuptial union (sanctified by going around the holy fire) and cementing the relationship. Upanayana (Sacred Thread Ceremony) is the gateway to focussed learning, by being initiated into the scriptures and, in particular, the all-important *Gayatri Mantra* from the *Rig Veda* as it says: 'We are aware of the domestic rituals. The rites they set out were fairly simple, some prescribed to be performed regularly and some on important occasions. In addition, the texts laid out rules related to the religious conduct of the household, typically specifying rites marking different stages of one's life cycle, which is described later. The *Agamas* (a class of instructional dialogues) were included in the set of Tantras. In the *Shaiva Agama*, for instance, Shiva addresses his consort Parvati, where Shiva is the male cosmic being and Shakti is the female creative energy.

Indeed, some Tantric rituals emphasise the worship of Shakti, as the creative energy of Shiva, since she projects the divine duality of masculine–feminine principles.

Standard Rituals

They aim at self-purification before worship and include *achamana* (drinking water from the palm to purify oneself), sprinkling holy water on one's head and limbs, and repeating mantras. Penitence for accumulated demerits (real or imagined) is

Devotees taking a dip during the Agni Tirtha, Rameshvaram , Tamil Nadu.

done through vow, bath, fast and worship on designated days, and specially on *Ekadasi* (the eleventh day after the new moon). Before divine blessings are sought, it is necessary to breathe life into an idol of god (or into a pot in abstract) through special ceremony and invocation *(prana pratistha).*

This is followed by the most commonly observed *puja* (worship) by offering flowers, leaves, fruits, milk, sweets, water, honey and incense, accompanied by chanting and singing to god. The ceremony usually culminates by sharing of *prasada* which had earlier been offered as the *naivedya* (ritual food to god). A water-filled earthen or brass pot – with mango leaves and coconut at its mouth – is installed at the place of worship or at the entry-point as an emblem of divinity and for its auspicious association with the Goddess of Wealth.

The Vedic *yajna* has been the culmination of all rituals, with elaborate laying of special bricks *(agni chayana),* designing the geometry of a highly elaborate platform *(vedi),* or hole *(kunda)* for the auspicious fire, and lighting up of the ceremonial fire *(havana)* to offer sacrifices through sacerdotal and sacramental rites as sanctified in the Vedas.

Ablution of the body at holy places and on holy occasions is a ritual believed to earn merit and absolve sin. Kartika Snana in September–October is a month-long religious observance where daily bath, followed by prayers and offerings to god, is considered beneficial. Makara Sankranti in December–January is another important occasion for ritual bathing accompanied by bonfire, ceremonial eating and considerable charity in Uttar Pradesh, Bihar and Bengal. Pongal Sankranti is a similar occasion celebrated in Tamil Nadu and Andhra Pradesh; Purna Kumbha Snana at the confluence of rivers Ganga and Yamuna in Allahabad and Ardha Kumbha Snana at Haridwar, Nasik and Ujjain, the latter occasions coming once in twelve and six years respectively, culminate in the holiest of ritual bathings, earning the highest merit. Purna Kumbha Snana and Ardha Kumbha Snana for an individual are widely-practised rituals, ranging from the procedure of the ten daily pious deeds, special rituals like daily *Trisandhya Ahnik* (three-fold meditations), and can go up to some recognised components of the primal cultures, like the one-legged stance or piercing the tongue during Charak *Puja* (mid-April).

Rituals, without exception, have clear structures where even a self-inflicted suffering may have its counterpart in deeper psychic satisfaction. The distinctive tantric practice aims at the arousing of 'coiled feminine energy' (Kundalini Shakti) as pure consciousness.

Life-Cycle Rituals

There are rituals and scarifices performed in an individual's own life cycle. These *samskaras* (sacraments), about forty in number (discussed later), may occur during conception and delivery; during one's life on earth as a child, as a youngster, and as an adult; right to the time of one's death and funeral ceremonies; and the observance of death anniversary. There are rites for marriage; for consecration of the womb; for birth; for naming of the child; for carrying him out for the first time to face the rising sun; for the child's first feeding with solid food; for the shaving of its head; for education; for investiture with the sacred thread; and rites for completion of studies. At a person's death, his sons would perform the rites of the pyre, and his spirit would be remembered with elaborate ceremonies for the ancestors, or those who have pre-deceased him.

The techniques of meditation, similarly, include rituals. There are *mudra*s (ritual gestures of the hands), *asana*s (bodily stances and postures), choice of timing and the whole preparation of the environment for meditation are ritually determined. Appropriate rites accompany seasonal events, pilgrimages, dedication of temple icons – indeed all occurrences, great and small, of personal and community life – to sanctify each occasion.

Ritual practices are of several kinds ranging from Bahya *Puja* (object or image worship) up to Manasa *Puja* (transcendental worship). Devotion to one's *ishta* (the choice) can be in the form or appearance in which reality presents itself to one's nature, growing in intensity of desire and singleness of mind through communication with one's *ishta devata* (chosen deity).

This is until it becomes transcendental worship: worship without object or distinction. This state of consciousness is marked by a sense of *shunya* (void). Rituals lead ultimately to concentration on *bindu* (the point), the centre at which all experience – all being – is compacted into its utmost concentration: to implode back into its origin.

Apart from the idea to propitiate the gods to make life easier, the sacraments are also used for social expression, as there are ceremonies for solemn occasions as well as for celebrations. In a broader sense, several rituals embrace temple premises, where the priest invokes the deity in the image that stands

A Hindu devotee gives in completely neither to the priest nor the idol, but to the God within himself.

The temple priest invokes the deity.

Tying of sacred robes and cloths to a tree is considered auspicious and is believed to fulfil the wishes of the devotees.

inside the sanctum sanctorum and the lay devotee stands at the threshold to have *darshan* (witness) of the god's presence in the temple's icons, where each image is pervaded with the *Antaryami* (Divine Spirit). In every ritual worship, either conducted by a priest or by the laity, a Hindu approaches neither a man nor an idol, but the god within oneself.

In the ritual world, the *Gayatri Mantra* (the hymn of sanctification recited by Brahmins during sunrise or most serious rites) and the *Beeja Mantra* (the seed-syllable used for initiation by guru under *Diksha*) hold the central context. The *Panchakshara Mantra* (*Om Namah Shivaya*, with five syllables) is homage to Shiva in Indian or Balinese rituals, where the rite is the priest's method of 'becoming Shiva' during the temple deeds. Similarly, the *Vaishnava Mantra* (*Om Namah Bhagavate Vasudevaya*, the twelve-syllable homage to Vishnu) relates each syllable to a month, and hence, to Time itself.

'Samskara' Rituals

Samskaras are rituals and sacrifices that a Hindu performs to remove hindrances, evil or otherwise, that tend to plague human life from time to time: by propitiating the gods. *Samskaras* may be for material gains, as well as for offspring, for land, for health, or even for winning disputes, contributing to happiness and prosperity, and attainment of social status. The rituals connected with *samskaras* involve both secular and religious ceremonies, using mantras (incantations) and multiple symbols. Out of some forty *samskaras*, the significance of a few major ones have been discussed below.

- **Garbhadana** or conception is the fervent prayer for a child performed to fulfil the parental duties in continuing the race.
- **Punsavana** or foetus protection is performed during the third or fourth month of pregnancy to invoke divine qualities in the child.
- **Simantonnayana** is performed in the seventh month by offering prayers for the healthy physical and mental growth of the child.
- **Jatakarma** is performed during childbirth to welcome the newborn into the family, by reciting mantra*s* for a healthy, long life both for the child and the mother.
- **Namakarana** or the naming ceremony is done according to scriptural procedures, along with

Mundan ceremony, a ritual of head shaving, is an important event.

Marriage ceremony being conducted by the priest in the presence of family members and relatives of the couple.

Nishkramana (exit) for taking the child outdoors for the first time at the age of four months.

- **Annaprasana** or giving the child cereals is the final childhood *samskara* for initiating the baby to solid food around the seventh or eighth month, according to the Grihya Sutra.
- **Upanayana** or the sacred thread ceremony is performed only for boys between six and twelve years old, amongst the upper echelons

of society. It symbolises a 'second' birth when they give up their young self and are 'born' into their new, spiritual self. It marks the transition to spiritual awareness and adult religious responsibilities. The priest invests the boy with a sacred thread over the shoulders and parents instruct him in pronouncing the *Gayatri Mantra*. For the young women in the South, such rituals are performed at the onset of menstruation.

Performing Sraddha: an annual ceremony to pay homage to one's ancestors.

- **Vivaha** or marriage is an important mid-life passage: deemed much more than a mere exchange of vows and rings. Since marriage is considered as a strong bonding between two families, that of the bride and the groom, many rites are performed in the presence of family deities, both before and during the nuptials, seeking blessings of the spiritual elements. The *misri* or ring ceremony is the initial ritual between the two families, which involves seeking of divine blessings, exchanging rings and garlands, and feeding each other *misri* (crystalline sugar) by way of confirming the engagement. The next is the *mehendi* (painting of hands and feet with henna) ceremony which signifies the strength of love between a couple. Nine planets are especially worshipped, in addition to a musical celebration.

The ceremony is performed by the priest, through the following rituals:

Satkara – Reception of the bridegroom, when the bride's mother blesses the boy with auspicious materials.

Madhuparka – Reception of the bridegroom at the altar when the bride's father blesses him with presentations.

Kanya Dana – The bride's father or his representative gives away the bride amidst the chanting of hymns.

Vivaha Havana – Sacred fire ceremony held in an atmosphere of purity and spirituality.

Pani Grahana – The groom accepts the hand of the bride as his lawfully wedded wife.

Pratijna – The bride leads the couple and circumambulates the fire, while taking solemn vows of loyalty, steadfast love and life-long fidelity to each other.

Shila Arohana – The bride's mother assists the bride to step on a stone slab and counsels her to prepare for a new life.

Laja Havana – The bride offers puffed rice as oblations into the sacred fire while keeping her palms together with the groom's.

Devotee at a temple gate.

Pradakshina – The couple circles the fire seven times and solemnises the marriage.

Saptapadi – The marriage-knot is tied between the groom's scarf and the bridal dress, while the couple takes seven steps together, each step symbolising: nourishment, strength, prosperity, happiness, progeny, long harmonious life and understanding.

Abhisheka – The couple meditates on the sun and the pole star who have been holy witnesses of their marriage.

Anna Prashana – The couple offers food into the fire and symbolically feeds each other to express mutual love and affection.

Ashirvada – The couple receives the blessings of their elders.

- After the death of a family member, the mourners go in procession to the burning or burial ground, as the practice may be. The closest relative of the deceased performs final rites: by lighting the funeral pyre and after cremation, collects the ashes to consign them eventually in a holy river. After a funeral, everyone attending undergoes a purifying bath. The immediate family remains in mourning for a set number of days, at the end of which there is a prayerful ceremony and often giving of gifts to the poor or to charities.

  The progeny carries out *sraddha,* an annual commemorative ceremony: to propitiate the departed ancestors, for three generations. The rituals comprise: *arghya* (water offering), *havana* (fire offering), *Brahmana bhojana* (the feeding of invited Brahmins), *pinda dana* (symbolic feeding of the ancestors), *dakshina* (money and other offerings) and *tarpana* (the actual act of propitiation).

Ceremonial Rituals

Ceremonies for rituals are many and varied, and do not always involve priests, especially the life cycle rituals which are confined to the family. Diverse totemic objects like *durba* (a form of grass), *til* (sesame seeds), lotus flower and sanctified water are used. Three important ceremonial acts, as mentioned earlier, include:

- **Puja** is the offering of flowers, *bel* leaves, fruits, sweet, milk and incense, besides water, accompanied by chanting of hymns and singing to the gods, with appropriate hand and body gestures. Interestingly, while *havana* (ritual fire) and *yajna* (fire sacrifice) were the original Vedic practices, *puja* was assimilated later in the non-Vedic times, especially from the Dravidian culture, as well as the Bhakti movement. A brass (or earthen) lamp is lit during the *puja* to invoke the benediction of the sun.
- **Kumbha** or the water-filled pot, with mango leaves and a coconut placed on top, represents the universe and water, *i.e.,* life. In many rituals, *kumbha* is worshipped in abstract, as the symbol of divinity.
- **Prana Pratishta** is the ritual performed with special ceremonies and invocations that breathes life into an idol as a god or goddess, and prepares it for worship. Again, there would be a subsequent *visarjana* (immersion), with complementary rituals to denude the divine

breath of life, thus observing a sanctified life cycle of the worshipped divinity.

Routine Rituals

There are a few rituals, followed as routines for civilised behaviour by Hindus, which delightfully conceal deeper significance and layers of meaning! A score of these routine and behavioural ritual patterns which are common are:

- **Salutation** in Sanskrit is usually known as Namaste, meaning 'I bow to you'. The folded palms placed on the chest are to recognise that the divinity is the same in all and bowing down of the head is a gracious recognition of the divinity in the person one meets.
- **Prostration before elders** or the touching of the feet is a sign of respect shown to elders, seeking their *sankalpa* (good wishes) and *ashirvada* (blessings) and receiving positive vibrations. Acknowledging the greatness of another is a tradition that reflects strong family ties, which has been one of India's enduring strengths.
- **Misdemeanour of touching papers, books and people with the feet** or the custom of not stepping on educational tools is a frequent reminder of the high esteem that is accorded to knowledge in Indian culture. Hindus show special reverence to books once a year on the day of Saraswati *Puja,* dedicated to the Goddess of Learning, and to vehicles and instruments dedicated to Vishwakarma, the God of Divine Construction. Touching another person with one's feet is akin to showing disrespect to the divinity within him or her.

- **Lighting a lamp at dawn/dusk at home** symbolises the kindling of knowledge. Just as light removes darkness, knowledge removes ignorance. By lighting the lamp, one bows down to knowledge as being the greatest of all forms of wealth.

- **Having a prayer room at home** to commune with the divinity and to rid oneself of false pride and possessiveness, as being earthly occupants of the divine property.

- **Applying 'tilak' on the forehead** invokes a feeling of sanctity in the wearer and is recognised as a religious symbol.

- **Applying the holy ash** or *bhasma* from the *havana* (ritual fire) on the forehead or on the upper arms or chest by ascetics, purifies and protects one from ill health.

- **Offering food to God before eating** and later partaking it as *prasada* is a daily ritualistic worship to acknowledge that man is a part, while the Lord is the totality.

- **Fasting** or *upavasa* in Sanskrit means, 'staying near', or in other words, the attainment of close proximity to the Lord.

- **Circumambulation** of the idol or *pradakshina* signifies that the Lord is at the centre of our lives and one goes about doing one's daily chores, recognising Him as the focal point.

- **Reverence for trees and plants** or showing respect to the life force in us, pervades all living beings, flora and fauna. Hence, they all are considered sacred especially as they support life on earth: by giving food, oxygen, clothing, shelter and medicine.

- **Ringing the bell in a temple** produces an auspicious sound: 'Om', the universal name of the Lord.

- **Worship of the 'kalasha'** involves the worship of the *kalasha* (the pot) containing water that symbolises the primordial water from which the entire creation has emerged, with the leaves and coconut representing creation.

- **Significance of the lotus** lies in the following reasons. One, the lotus blooms with the rising sun and closes its petals at night. Similarly, our minds open up and expand with the light of knowledge. Two, the lotus leaf never gets wet even though it is always in water. It symbolises the *Jnani* (the man of wisdom) who remains unaffected by the world of sorrow and change. Three, a lotus emerges from the navel of Vishnu, with Brahma originating from it to create the world. Hence, the lotus symbolises the link between the Creator and creation.

- **Worship of the 'tulsi'** is considered most sacred and self-purifying. The *tulsi* can be used, washed and re-used. It has great medicinal value and cures many ailments including common cold

  Blowing of the conch or the primordial sound of 'Om' emanates from the *shankhu* (conch), recalling the auspicious sound chanted by the Lord before creating the world. In small villages, people who cannot make it to the temple are reminded to stop wherever they are, take a break from their work and mentally bow to the Lord.

- **Uttering 'shanti'** or peace, thrice, after a prayer chant, invokes the natural state of being as the

Prayers offered during Deepavali, the Festival of Lights.

adhibhautik (material), *adhidaivik* (physical) and *adhyatmic* (spiritual) attributes are appeased. It is believed that what is repeated thrice comes true, as is the oath on truth in a court of law.

- **Offering a coconut** on any occasion like weddings, festivals, using a new vehicle, entering a new house or apartment, by breaking it, symbolises the breaking of the human ego. The juice within represents *vasana* (the inner desires), which is then offered to the Lord, along with the white kernel: the mind. In the traditional *abhisheka* (enthronement) ritual, done in all temples and homes for the presiding deities, several ritual materials are poured over the deity like milk, curd, honey, sandal paste, holy ash and tender coconut water. Each material carries a specific significance of bestowing certain benefits on the worshippers.

- **Chanting 'Om'** marks the beginning of all auspicious actions and is even used as part of

Reaching for the temple-bell.

swah, as sanctified in the *Gayatri Mantra*). The Lord is in all these and beyond.

- **Performing 'arati'** at the end of every ritual worship or even while welcoming an honoured guest is accompanied by the ringing of the bell, singing of prayers, playing of musical instruments and clapping of the hands. It is performed with *shodasha upacharas* (sixteen totemic objects), one after the other, like the earthen lamp (to behold the beautiful form of the Lord), camphor (burning of all our desires without leaving a trace), fruits, delicacies, conch, etc. The flame of the *arati* turns our attention to the very source of all light, such as the sun (the presiding deity of intellect), moon (that of the mind) and fire (that of speech). Once the *arati* is over, we place our stretched palms over the flame and then touch our eyes as well as the head, implying the prayer: 'May the light that illumines the Lord brighten my vision; may my vision be divine; and my thoughts noble and beautiful.'

Temple Rituals

All the aforesaid rituals find their culmination in the temple and get merged one way or the other. Transposed to the divinity, rituals take the form of entirely anthropomorphic worship. The individual's daily cycle of rituals, for instance, are reiterated for the icon, where the images of deities are treated with deeply reverential prayers and ceremonies are held: beginning from waking up of the deity in the morning, its ablution; dressing up, feeding, and continuing up to *arati* with lamps and conch-blowing, and finally, the night's rest.

a greeting. It is one of the most chanted sound symbols in India. 'Om' starts all mantras and Vedic prayers. Made up of 'O' (phonetically as in 'around'), 'U' (as in 'put') and 'M' (as in 'mum'), the three letters symbolise three states (waking, slumber and dream); three deities (Brahma, Vishnu and Shiva); three Vedas (*Rig, Yajur* and *Sama);* and three worlds (*bhuh, bhuvah* and

A traditional puja thali *typically containing a lamp, coconut, grains, tulsi leaves, ghee, sandalwood paste, vermilion.*

The Hindu temple (*devalaya*) has architecturally the Vedic *rite de passage*, which creates a psychological separation of the worshipper from his habitual concerns, prior to his engaging in the sacrifice. The ritual manuals of Vishnu often distinguish his four icons: the ceremonial image conforming precisely to iconography; the complementary image with the god's consort (Lakshmi); the image for festive processions; and the image for worship by lay devotees.

The medieval Shiva texts on practical religion (*agamas*) lay down the ritual preparation for the stages of meditation. As stated earlier, the Vedas had not promulgated gods and their temples. It was the ritual itself, consisting of mantras and mudras – pronounced and performed by priests (and initiated laymen) – that engendered the Hindu religious experience. The words built up partially anthropomorphic images of elements and psychological forces.

Later on, many components of these metaphors were to find concrete expression in monumental temples and artistic representations of the gods: in stone, metal and earth. Meanwhile, rituals have continued to serve their all-important purpose: of renewing one's connections with the life force and with the godhead in order to retain zest and vitality in living. Rituals have fulfilled a social function: to bind together large groups of believers, linking different units of society within a generation and several generations within a race, as religion came early to people only in the form of rituals with a meaning. Rituals have also served a historical function: to bind the present with the past and provide a visible continuity for religion.

Devotees at Tirumala in Tirupati, Andhra Pradesh, shown in the act of coconut breaking, symbolising the breaking of the human ego.

Chapter Four

Social Ethics

Social Ethics

Rituals, integral to the Hindu way of noble living, are perhaps more in number in Hinduism than in other religions. As a part of life, they come naturally to all Hindus, almost as instincts.

Ascetic on his quest for knowledge. Hinduism does not lay down any specific approach to reach God. Jnana, karma and bhakti are the various paths.

Hinduism is a product of many races and cultures: contributing to the extraordinary complexity of India's society and religion. Since the term Hindu was derived from the Sindhu River (the Indus), Persians referred to India, as the land beyond the Sindhu. Hinduism would thus appear to be a generic term, meaning the society and religions of the people in India. Fortunately, there is greater unity in Hinduism, as it has evolved over centuries and ensured the preservation of the Indian unity.

The complex social ethics of Hinduism laid down that the duties of a person differ, depending on the temperament of the person concerned and the stage of his career. There are, of course, some universal values like truth, kindness and love, which are considered to be every human being's duty, but man's more specific pursuits would be relative to his age and temperament. So renunciation and what is sometimes called 'other-worldliness' are by no means the only Hindu values.

Active material service is as much a part of Hindu life as contemplation and spirituality. Even the approach to the Supreme may be either through *jnana* (knowledge), or through karma (action), or with the help of bhakti (devotion). Those who do not find prayers necessary for fulfilling their life's obligations may approach God through good deeds. For others, prayers may constitute a vital part of their approach and the path of devotion may be the best suited one. A proper appreciation of the Hindu societal system of values lead unambiguously to the basic assumption of 'Many ways to God', not espoused in most other religions. A major tenet of Hinduism is to accept as religion whatever holds the key to one's own and others' living and growing. Religion, in that sense, is a universal force that enjoins the general welfare of all.

The ten signs of religiosity laid down by the law-giver Manu (AD 100–300) are—patience, tolerance, forbearance, non-covetousness, cleanliness, control of senses, intelligence, knowledge, truthfulness and equanimity. Anyone professing them would be called religious, whatever be the given faith.

Basic Code of Conduct

Social observances can be: *lokachara* (popularly accepted norms of behaviour) or *shastrachara* (scriptural codes of behaviour). The first set of rules lay down the socially accepted rules without any formal sanction of the scriptures while the latter fall back upon strict support from the books of law. Few *lokachara*s and *shastrachara*s are concerned not only with general codes of conduct (such as honesty, unselfish work, kindness and love), but also with details of formal behaviour often specifying performance of rituals. Both popular and scriptural codes are, in the ultimate

A believer makes a humble offer in earnest devotion.

analysis, *bahya* (external), permitting anyone, feeling temperamentally in conflict with the detailed observance, not to be bound by them. *Bauls* (mendicant singers) and members of certain Bhakti schools, for instance, often declare their

In the Guru-Shishya Parampara, *which traces its lineage to Vedic times, the Guru not only imparted teachings on Hindu ideals to his disciples, but also trained them to be critical of the prevailing social and religious codes of conduct.*

rejection of these rituals: without denying the basic Hindu ideals.

At times, gurus (teachers) have recommended to their disciples the non-performance of some conventional rites, but this has not made them any less Hindu, provided that the basic Hindu ideals and the fundamental social codes of conduct have not been denied. Indeed, the uniting factor among the enormous variety of religious beliefs and ceremonies, which one finds in Hinduism, has been a belief in such a basic code of behaviour, namely, selfless work, detachment, honesty and love, as sanctioned in the Bhagavad Gita.

In the conduct of religious worship, Hinduism is very liberal. Since one may try to reach God through *jnana* or karma or bhakti, all approaches are equally valid. Hinduism denies the existence of any exclusive way of reaching God, and allows the details of religious performance of rituals to vary from person to person, as also their religious assumptions. *Mahima Stotra* (hymn of praise) reveals the essence of Hinduism in the following lines:

> All these paths, O Lord, like Veda, Samkhya, Yoga,
> Pasupata and Vaishnava, lead to but to You, as does
> the winding river at last merges with the sea.

Many regard this as the central message of Hinduism, viewing God as infinite, omniscient, omnipotent and omnipresent, but appearing to be different to different people.

Professional Hierarchy ('Varna')

Rules of family conduct and social obligations were compiled in the *Manu Samhita* (Code of Manu), as related to professional hierarchy *(varna)* and the phases of life *(ashrams)*. Scientifically linked to the natural ability for work, *varna* became a four-fold division as a standard means of classifying the population as early as 600 BC. In an idealistic view, people, who are by nature simple, large-hearted and kind to others, would engage themselves in the pursuit of higher thoughts, become visionaries for civilisation and be termed Brahmins. Those who are brave and fearless would take on the role of protecting others in the society, administer the state and be termed Kshatriyas. Those who have a penchant for hard work and enterprising ability, would hold on to commerce and business activities, provide the means of livelihood to others, and be termed Vaishyas. Others, who may lack ability or inclination to either protect or nurture

Manu Maharani Temple, Manali, Himachal Pradesh. Manu codified the varna *system.*

the society, would still stand and serve, and be called the Shudras.

Initially, attributes assumed in the above objective classification were: humanitarian virtues *(sattvah);* enterprising capability *(rajah);* and reluctance for hard work *(tamah),* in a mix-and-match order, as sanctified in the highly venerated treatise the Bhagavad Gita: 'Four hierarchies are created by Me, according to anyone's qualities and working nature.'

Over time, the priestly Brahmins, the warring Kshatriyas, the trading community of Vaishyas, and the farmers and labourers as Shudras found themselves falling into 'castes' (a name coined by the Portuguese) and became tenable only by heredity. Caste membership started being defined simply by birth and fluidity of movement from one caste to another ceased to be permissible.

This gave rise to community groups *(jatis)* who were all part of local or regional hierarchies. While individuals could not move up the social scale, groups aspired to gain recognition as high social rungs by adopting practices and occupations that were hereditary.

Phases in Life (Ashram)

The Hindu society, regardless of professional hierarchy, expected life to run through four phases: as celibate (in *Brahmacharya*); as family man (in *Garhasthya*); as recluse (in *Banaprastha*) and as hermit (in *Sannyas*). The name *ashram,* given to these phases, came from the concept of voluntarily contributing one's fruit of labour *(shram)* to the upkeep of family and community, and thereby helping them to grow in an ideal society. The phases also related to the study of

Swami Vivekananda upheld the ideals of the Vedanta.

also laid down the *purushartha* (goals of attainment) in an individual's life. The aims would be to gain: *dharma* (religious attainment), *artha* (material benefit), *kama* (emotional satisfaction), and *moksha* (ultimate salvation).

The first three are applicable to an ordinary mortal who obviously leans towards physical and mental enjoyment. But these begin with a religious binding, which can regulate life and channelise energies towards happiness and wisdom. On the contrary, a mindless pursuit of only material and sentient comforts can lead to dissoluteness and grief; a statement valid even to this day.

This earlier integration trigerred a social revolution and created a dominant society which gave Hinduism a unity at the top. It was no doubt a great achievement for that period. But beneath the top layer was the sizeable body of unrelated social units: grouped together as 'castes', which followed their own laws and customs, without referring to the Hindu philosophy. Besides, there were countless 'untouchables' and other backward classes who were separated from the upper echelons of the Hindu social life.

The integration that is taking place now is a consummation and fulfilment of the great vision that existed in the centuries before the Buddha and continued till the early Christian millennium. The continued existence of Hindu society, long after political power disappeared from the Hindu monarchs and the machinery of reorganisation became dysfunctional, is a miracle in history. In spite of internal and external pressures, the society continued to maintain its institutions and structures, before becoming, in the recent centuries,

Vedic scriptures. First, the celibate phase should see the disciples learn and remember properly the *mantras* (hymns) from the gurus. The family phase would permit the application of the practical aspects (Brahman).

The retired phase should allow ample time to inquire into the philosophy of the rites *(aranyak)*. Finally, if one were inclined to leave everything and become a hermit, one should engage completely in the pursuit of knowledge of the Brahman and Atman.

It would appear that religion was inseparable from living in early society where the Vedic seers immobile, fragmented and, to a degree, immune to progressive ideas. Every new generation saw further fragmentation and newer sects.

Revival of Vedanta

While the relative ossification of castes and community groups led to much discontent, leading to undesirable social disabilities and divisiveness, the impact of the West at the beginning of the nineteenth century revived the spirit of the Hindu society. Two pioneers who spearheaded the revival are discussed below.

Raja Ram Mohan Roy (1774–1833)

As a champion of monotheism, he advocated in his *Tuhfat' ul-muhwahhiddin* (A Gift to Monotheists) in 1804, the egalitarian view that man has a natural tendency to worship one God without visible form and that priests for their own profit, promote other forms of worship. In 1815, he published *Vedanta Grantha,* consisting of commentaries on *Brahma-Sutras* (mainly based on Samkara's) followed by *Vedanta Sara.* He often used the design of the universe as an argument for the existence of God, in the manner of European rational theism and saw a close connection between true belief and morality. Unlike Samkara, Ram Mohan did not see Vedanta as the religion of an elite, but held that householders can and should know Brahman.

Swami Vivekanada (1863–1902)

He considered that the common heritage of all Indians and the foundation of Hinduism was the Vedanta. It held the key to India's identity and was the source of India's greatness in the past, and of her confidence

Raja Ram Mohan Roy, emphasised on monotheism.

for the future. According to him, *Advaita Vedanta* offered the only religion which agreed with and went further than modern researches in the West. Using Vedanta as a base for the unity underlying Indian culture, he found it as the befitting answer to the challenge of foreign values, a view, given more weight later by Dr S. Radhakrishnan.

Reformation

The Hindu reformation was a major development of that period, as it succeeded to transform a moribund society through vigorous social action as well as through an enabling process of legislations. There were three streams of reformation movements:

Brahmo Samaj

Begun by Raja Ram Mohan Roy in Calcutta in 1828 and resurrected by Debendranath Tagore in 1843, it spearheaded many reformist activities that gathered momentum under Keshub Chandra Sen, a dynamic leader. Today, there are some eighty branches of its three groups in India and thirty-four abroad.

Ramakrishna Mission

Founded by Sri Ramakrishna's most ardent disciple Swami Vivekananda outside Calcutta in 1897, it provides devoted service to the people. Delving deep into philosophy and literature, Vivekananda spread the message of love and spirituality, and inspired a whole generation of leaders and people in many parts of the world.

Sri Ramakrishna, the guru of Swami Vivekananda, stressed that God is one and that various religions are merely different paths to reach Him.

The mind of the Indian society was deeply influenced by these reformist events. The abolition of 'untouchability' was a plank in Mahatma Gandhi's programme, which attempted to bring the lower castes – discriminated against by the upper ones – within the fold by calling them 'God's children' (Harijan). This did not produce the desired results and 'schedules' of backward castes have been drawn to provide succour.

The more secular term 'the oppressed' (Dalit) is presently in use. Since Independence, in 1947, several affirmative actions have been undertaken to provide up to 30 per cent reservations of jobs in government-run institutions and in further education, leading to professional qualifications for these groups. Members of the 'scheduled castes' and 'scheduled tribes' are found in all important positions in the Indian economy.

Arya Samaj

Founded by Dayanand Saraswati in Bombay in 1875, it differed from tradition by giving less importance to Puranic gods, denouncing image worship and extolling the chanting of Vedic mantras. Aiming mainly at social reforms, it questioned child marriages, advocated women's education and supported widow remarriages. Presently, it has over 3,000 branches today in India and abroad.

Genuine regard for the feminine intellect has been enshrined in many scintillating dialogues quoted in the scriptures, as in the conversation between Yajnavalkya and his learned consort Maitreyee on the ephemera of life and the significance of *amrita* (the eternal knowledge). There were many Vedic women like Gargi who contributed their erudition in composing hymns.

Down the ages, there has been a downgrading of gender values, but nearer our time, the participation of women in the freedom struggle has been remarkably large, giving rise to many luminaries who led the movement. Equal status for women has been a demand raised over many decades, resulting in substantial participation of women in many spheres, including their spectacular entry in the village Panchayats. Changes in marriage law, women's right to property and many other reforms have been the outcome of contemporary liberal thinking.

The Indian transformation, today, is basically a fulfilment, discarding many customs and practices associated with the Hindus for centuries. Hindu life has also broadened its horizons, gradually incorporating in the society millions who were kept out and held down by harsh social practices.

Due to these changes, the Hindus stand forth today as a society informed by progressive ideas, based on equality, where women have the same rights as men, where men are no longer tied down by castes, and where social relations are not being continuously fragmented. One awaits the Vedic wisdom to shine forth again and enlighten the society of present times.

Mahatma Gandhi attempted to eliminate caste distinction and named the untouchables Harijans or *'God's children'* .

Chapter Five
Consciousness

Consciousness

Hinduism is a religious and cultural tradition which combines an enormous variety of beliefs and practices and incorporates, integrates and ultimately interprets religion not as a dogma about God, but as the state of consciousness of the Divine.

Obeissance to a tree. Hinduism is an agglomeration of a variety of beliefs and pratices.

Several ideas and beliefs run like a thread through Hinduism providing its psychological and intellectual staple. According to Dr S. Radhakrishnan, religion for the Hindu

> ... is not an idea but a power, not an intellectual proposition but a life conviction. Religion is consciousness of ultimate reality, not a theory about God.

In a major sense, Hinduism is a religious and cultural platform enriched by many beliefs and practices that have merged together down the ages and have ultimately created a *weltanschauung*, a common view of the world. Yet, there is no Hindu organisation – similar to the Catholic Church – with the authority to define belief or establish official practice.

Because the religion is so ancient, one can trace within Hinduism, the development of the human mind in its struggles to understand the mysteries of life. According to the *Brihadaranyaka Upanishad*:

This immutable one is never seen, but is the witness;

It is never heard, but is the hearer;

It is never thought about, but is the thinker;

It is never known, but is the knower,

There is no other witness but this ...

Perhaps mankind's first attempt at a psychological analysis occurred in the Samkhya philosophy, propounded by Sage Kapila. Indirectly, the doctrines of reincarnation, non-sensory perception and the superconscious have profound repercussions on the nature of the psyche and consciousness. Western psychology treats the unconscious, the pre-conscious and the conscious as products of matter and the individual as a temporary cohesion of these functions. Hindu psychology, in contrast,

A devotee praying at Lord Nataraja Temple, Chidambaram, Tamil Nadu. Meditation and prayer provides the laity with a religious insight or darshana.

Sri Aurobindo held that man can attain the Supreme Consciousness by awakening the chakras.

sees the individual as a permanent manifestation of consciousness, functioning through and structuring the limitations of mind and personality, and doing so in various bodies through time. The evolution of human species is, to that extent, the emergence of consciousness. The purpose of the *darshanas* is to explain, enhance and facilitate this evolution.

The epic Mahabharata defines ten tenets as the embodiment of *dharma* (religion): good name; self-control; purity of mind and body; simplicity; endurance; resoluteness of character; giving and sharing; austerities; and continence. In religious thinking, these tenets are nearly synonymous with the five patterns of behaviour: non-violence; attitude of equanimity; peace and tranquility; lack of aggression and cruelty; and absence of envy. In this sense, Hinduism represents the order inherent in human life: essentially secular rather than religious, and independent of any revelation or commandment of God.

Some important opinions or beliefs in the Hindu mind are discussed here.

Darshana (view)

Apart from representing different philosophies such as Yoga or Vedanta, *darshanas* or 'views' are used commonly to describe the sight of the deity by the laity in a temple. Equally, it may apply to religious insight gained through meditation and prayer. Hence, the *Rig Veda* explains:

> Who is the Being to whom we should offer our worship and prayer? ... He who is the giver of knowledge and strength, whom the whole world worships, whose command all learned people obey, whose house is immortality, whose shadow is death – He it is to whom we shall offer our prayers and worship.

To quote the *Taittiriya Upanishad*:

> The self (Atman) is not attained through intellectual discourse, or, through much learning. Only those who long for the Truth, with their whole heart, gain it. To such ones, the Self reveals its own nature.

The six systems of Hindu philosophy (Nyaya, Vaisheshika, Samkhya, Yoga, Mimamsa and

Vedanta), as aforesaid, are known as *darshanas*: meaning view, vision, seeing or viewpoint.

The six systems embrace several different concepts of *Ishvara* (God) with varied names that are not really deities, but are various aspects of an Infinite Being. This is also because no one concept can appeal to everybody's mind, because individuals are at different stages of evolution, capacity and understanding. Mimamsa makes no mention of a deity. Samkhya takes an agnostic attitude, saying: 'God is not proved', but not denying God. Yoga of Sage Patanjali does not make the system dependent upon a deity, but advises that it is a useful concept, though remaining very different from the Christian concept of God. The various schools of Vedanta and Yoga cover most theological concepts of divinity and, eventually, transcend them all!

The ideas common to all the *darshanas* range from absolutely real, to provisionally real, to a delusion! The three-tiered attitude is beautifully expressed in the Ramayana:

O Lord, when I think of myself with the body, I look upon You as my master and myself as Your servant. When I think of myself as the individual soul, I regard You as the Infinite Whole and myself as Your part. When I look upon myself as the Spirit transcending all limitations, my individuality is lost in You and I realise that I am verily Yourself.

Evolution of Consciousness

The evolution of consciousness: from the relative to the absolute, from ignorance to knowledge, from mortality to immortality, from obscurity to clarity, from doubt to truth, from error to righteousness: is a constant theme of Hindu *Darshanas*. According to the Vaisheshika School, there are fourteen planes of consciousness through which the life process evolves. The first four planes are: the cell-divided protozoa, the seed-born plants, the egg-born animals and the womb-born mammals. Man is the highest form of the womb-born, as he is self-conscious, stands upright, can speak and possess the *chakras* (subtle centres) through which consciousness can evolve to the highest, as envisaged by Sri Aurobindo. But in terms of spiritual development, ordinary man is at the fifth (and lowest) plane: gross understanding, engrossed in sense-life, self-centred and materialistic. The sixth and seventh planes belong to ignorance, but with intimations of inquiry and knowledge.

Six chakras running across the spine are the energy centres of the human body.

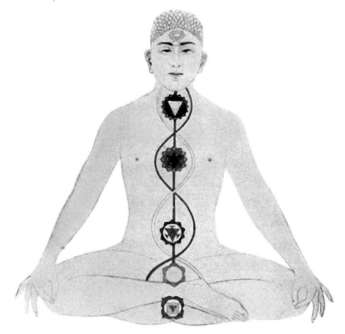

The seventh and eighth planes are the beginnings of higher evolution, when the faculties of superior intelligence, logic and reason are manifest. In the ninth plane, development of these faculties results in dual philosophies that reveal more of the reality, with 'God' seen as the utterly other, and the world as absolutely real. The tenth plane is a state of knowledge of the laws of civil life and insight into the moral order. The concept of God as a benign creator and father is appropriate at this stage, as intimately related to individuals, but in heaven.

In the eleventh plane, there is a higher understanding, control of the internal energies and sharpening of the intelligence. With the study of philosophy along with the practice of Yoga, concepts of God are varied and subtle, but dualism is still the reality. God is no longer seen as 'somewhere other', but equivalent to the human soul in some way. This is the dawn of qualified non-dualism.

In a fascinating sojourn towards Godhead, nature is understood and the higher mind is developed in the twelfth plane, when there is an intuitive understanding of the soul and God: as sparks are to the flame or a drop of water is to a lake. The moral and ethical nature, the intelligence and creativity are all at peak and the animal nature is totally subdued.

In the penultimate plane, there is a realisation of God and a transcendental state of love and bliss in states of trance, often accompanied by psychic powers such as saints of all religions have demonstrated. The final plane is complete self-realisation or enlightenment: with actual identity with Brahman, sans any duality. Having reached this plane all is 'One' and there is no longer any

need for evolution. The body may continue to live till the past karma is spent, but there is no rebirth. An individual, free from Karmic impediments, may experience all the planes in a single lifetime and win *moksha*.

Karma (effect of earlier actions)

According to this idea, which is termed as Karmic by the West, every person or animal has a self (Atman), which has existed without beginning. Every deed leaves an indelible mark on that self, which is carried forward into the next life and leaves an overall imprint on each person's self as: controlling the nature of one's next birth (animal, human or even God); determining the family one would be born into, if human; regulating the length of the next life; and resolving the good or bad experience that the self will experience. It does not, however, imply a fatalistic belief that the nature of action in this life is unimportant. Rather, it suggests that the path followed by the individual in the present life is vital to the nature of one's next life, and ultimately a determinant to gain release from this world. Karma, commonly understood as above, is a moral law, which makes the individual *(jiva)* wholly responsible for the situations and circumstances of life he is succumbed to. It is in stark contrast to popular opinion, which sees the individual as a product of the past and the environment or as the will of God.

On a more mature view, karma also means that the individual has a history going back to the dawn of life on the planet. Our consciousness has evolved from several life forms, replicating by cell division, to the seed-born, to the egg-born, then to the womb-born animal, and finally, to the human form. Consciousness continues to evolve in each one of us, until the Atman is realised. Each *jiva* is a reservoir of potentials that can only become actual under the right conditions and in the right time, which requires transmigration from one life form to another: then from one human body to another.

Punarjanma (rebirth)

Belief in the transmigration of souls in a perennial cycle of rebirth has been a distinctive thought in the entire Indian culture. Beginning from the Upanishads of the seventh century BC, when the doctrine of karma first appeared, the belief has endured and remained valid in Buddhism and Jainism. Gradually, greater consciousness is expressed, as the primeval amoeba becomes Man (derived from Manas, the thinker). When an individual realises that their intrinsic nature has become the Supreme Consciousness, there is no longer any need to remain evolving.

This is recapitulated in the famous dictum in the Bhagavad Gita:

> As one discards the worn-out clothes to don the new ones, so does the human being leave behind his mortal body and adopt a novel one!

The world is an appearance that makes the play of an evolving *jiva* possible. On the one hand, nature urges this evolution possible forward, while at the same time, it produces obstacles to an easy and swift consummation. This is the nature of the world!

Meditation helps in controlling the mind.

Ahimsa (non-violence)

The belief in transmigration might have encouraged the doctrine of non-violence or non-injury (ahimsa). The belief in rebirth implies that all living things and creatures of the spirit – people, gods, animals, even worms – possess the same essential soul. Hence, the paramount need is to exercise charity and compassion, as revealed in the following lines from the *Brihadaranyaka Upanishad*:

> Subdue the senses, do acts of charity, be compassionate. Practise these three virtues—control of the senses, charity and compassion.

In a broader sense, morals and ethics, relating to human behaviour, are recognised as part of the overall spiritual development. They are not ends in themselves, but means to the development of a

A state of physical and mental tranquillity and poise is attained by practising Yogasana.

superior intellect by which one can appreciate the subtle nuances of philosophy, and make possible an environment in which a righteous life can be lived. Further, morals of right action are rooted in the *rita* (cosmic order) by which the harmony of the universe is maintained. One should, therefore, seek to live in harmony with the cosmic order, if one wants to understand it and live life. *Yamas* and *niyamas* (morals and ethics) are the pre-requisites for the practice of all Yogas.

Yoga

Yoga visualises specific directions for actualising the human potential for release from the cycle of rebirth and attaining the Godhead. The basic systems of meditation are contextualised in the Bhagavad Gita and can be viewed as four paths to the goal of uniting the human spirit with God, which is regarded as one of the most realistic systems of thought and training ever set up by the human mind. Semantically, Yoga

is used for union, fortune, contribution, meeting, relationship, meditation or addition. Philosophically, it is the effort to unite the self with the Supreme Being, with concentration as the basis of meditation. To quote Patanjali, the father of *Yoga Shastra:* 'Yoga is controlling the nature of mind.' The four major systems of meditation are discussed below.

Jnana Yoga (System of Knowledge)

One should have a strong reflective bend of mind and be able to follow the steep path to oneness with Godhead through knowledge. It is the process of converting intellectual knowledge into practical wisdom. As a means to obtain the highest meditative state and inner knowledge, it refers to the process of meditation that leads to wisdom through self-enquiry and self-realisation. Its components are: not believing but realising; self-awareness, leading to self-analysis; experiencing knowledge; realising the innermost personal nature; developing intuitive wisdom; and experiencing inner unity and tranquility.

Bhakti Yoga (System of Devotion)

The most popular of the four, one strives not to identify with God, but to adore God with every pore of one's being. It involves reposing total faith in God or the Supreme Consciousness in any of the forms: Rama, Krishna, Christ, Mohammed, Buddha or a guru. There has to be strong emotional bonding with the object of faith, as the flow of emotional energy brings forth the purification of the inner self. Continuous meditation gradually decreases the ego, prevents distractions and fickleness of mind, making the practitioner lose self-identity and becoming one with the object of faith: a state of self-realisation.

Karma Yoga (System of Righteous Work)

As a path of devotion to work, it is to render deeds selflessly and act for God's sake rather than one's own. Non-attachment with the work and absence of attachment to rewards and incentives are the hallmarks of this difficult state. Initially, the existing sense of ego and attachment to the fruits of one's efforts are to be shed and work should become akin to the worship of God. As the deeds become spiritual, one becomes a yogi, achieving stability of mind in all conditions and actions representing God's will. According to the Bhagavad Gita: 'One must perform every action sacramentally and be free of one's attachments to the outcome.'

Raja Yoga (System of Psychosomatic Experiments)

As a comprehensive Yoga system, it deals with the refinement of human behaviour and personality. It conducts mental exercises and observes their subjective effects on the body through the practice of: *yamas* (restraints) and *niyamas* (disciplines); attainment of physical health and vitality through *asanas* (postures) and *pranayamas* (special breathing and awakening techniques); management of mental and emotional conflicts; development of awareness through *pratyahara* (sensory withdrawal) and *dharna* (concentration on object); and developing the creative aspect of consciousness for transcendental awareness through *dhyana* (meditation) and *samadhi* (salvation, by absorption in the universal identity). These steps are also collectively termed as Patanjali's Ashtanga Yoga of eight limbs.

The point of connection in the above-mentioned systems of meditation is Yoga viewed as the 'way': Jnana Yoga leads to union through discernment; Bhakti Yoga lays the path of union through love and devotion; Karma Yoga is the way of salvation; and Raja Yoga is the path of realisation through meditation. There is also a fifth form, Hatha Yoga in tantric concept, which develops psychosomatic forces towards the ultimate goal of salvation. The five other systems of Yoga are:

- **Kriya Yoga** or the System of Activity originated in antiquity and evolved through experience. There are about twenty practices prescribed in several tantric texts. It purposely creates activity and awakening in consciousness, when all faculties are harmonised and flower to their full potential.
- **Swara Yoga** or the System of Sound is the science of a complete study, observation, control and manipulation of *swara* (breath). It aims at realising cosmic consciousness through control and manipulation of breath.
- **Mantra Yoga** or the System of Chanting originated in Vedic sciences and also in the Tantras. It aims at only chanting and singing Vedic verses to achieve salvation or union with the Supreme Consciousness.
- **Hatha Yoga** or the System of Postures is the catalyst to the awakening of the physical as well as mental energy that govern our lives. It is a popular Yoga that includes Yogic *asanas* (Yoga positions), together with six *shatkarmas* (physical and mental detoxification techniques); *mudras* and *bandhas* (psychosomatic energy-

release techniques); and *pranayamas* (special techniques of breathing and awakening). Fine tuning of the human personality at increasingly subtle levels leads to higher states of awareness and meditation.

- **Kundalini Yoga** or the System of Psychic Centres is taken from the Tantras. It is concerned with the awakening of the *chakras* (psychic centres) that are presumed to exist in every human body; and are spread linearly from the bottom of the spinal chord and rising up to the *bindu* (point) at the bottom of *sahasra* (cerebellum): the brain. The six main *chakras*, in the ascending order, are: *Muladhara, Swadhistana, Manipura, Anahata, Vishuddhi* and *Ajna*.

The human mind is made up of subtle layers: progressively associated with higher levels of consciousness, related to these *chakras*. The latter progress from the animal mind, then to the instinctive realms, and finally, to the sublime heights of consciousness. Awakening the higher-level *chakras* involves deep concentration on these psychic centres and forcing their arousal. *Asanas, pranayamas, mudras* and *bandhas* as well as other Yogas like Mantra Yoga are used to stimulate the awakening.

Patanjali, while describing the hindrances against Yoga practice in his magnum opus *Yoga Darshana*, states:

> ... beware of the nine *Yogamalas* (interruptions), namely, *Vyadhi* (physical ailments); *Stan* (lack of the needed ability for the pratices of Yoga); *Samshay* (misapprehensions about yogic pratices); *Prasada* (unwillingness to follow rules and regulations); *Alasya* (lethargy in not attempting such practices); *Aviate* (disinterest in Yoga due to preoccupation elsewhere); *Bhranti Darshana* (misconceptions about the details of the pratices of Yoga); *Alabdha Bhoomikatya* (concentration not being developed to the desired extent in spite of the yogic practices); and *Anavasthi Tatya* (non-retention of concentration despite reaching a certain level).

Hindu beliefs and practices cover the complete spectrum from the metaphysical to the purely physical in a manner that is not found in any other faith or way of life.

The believer aspires to reach out to the Supreme and, ultimately, become one with Him. True Hindu consciousness dwells here.

Dr S. Radhakrishnan put it all in a nutshell in the refrain: 'It does not matter what conception of God we adopt, so long as we keep up a perpetual search for truth.'

Facing page: *Pranayam enables a yogi to attain mental poise and enhance his power of concentration.*

Chapter Six
Literature

Literature

The Rig Veda Samhita contains more than ten thousand verses. Encompassing a wide spectrum of beliefs, it expresses the wonder of a people fully awakened to the beauty, grandeur, majesty and mystery of nature.

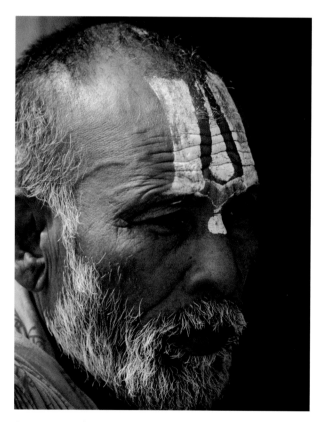

Portrait of a Hindu sadhu.

Since the Vedic times, Hinduism has seen the flourishing of an astonishing amount of literature, most of it resplendent with the highest thoughts and imagination. The Vedic religion, at its zenith in the second millennium BC, showed a profound sensitivity to the diversity of existence and environment, and a strong intellectual need to organise and unify them, which inspired much of the poetry of the Vedas. The Vedic poets' creativity and power of evocation tended to crystallise all aspects of experience into individual groupings of symbols in their works.

Vedas

The Vedas (Book of Knowledge), composed between 3000 BC and 2500 BC, have been called a vast 'smorgasbord': offering such a spectrum of beliefs that there is something for everyone at all levels of evolution, tastes and powers of digestion. There are four Vedas—*Rig, Yajur, Sama* and *Atharva*—not written for centuries after they were originally

An Indian manuscript throwing light on Hindu religious beliefs.

composed, but transmitted orally. Each is divided into three sections: *Samhitas* (collection of mantras and hymns), *Brahmanas* (collection of religious and ritual formulae) and *Aranyakas* (forest books). Each of them, in turn, is divided into two: *Karma Kanda* (action section) comprising rituals, rites, hymns, duties, sacrifices and sciences; and *Vidya Khanda* (knowledge section) laying down the philosophy. Attached to each *Brahmana* is an Upanishad (mystical doctrine).

While *Samhitas* and *Brahmanas* are highly revered as *shrutis* (heard from divine sources), the Upanishads are termed as *smritis* (memorised or learnt). In general, a *Samhita* has the earliest hymns addressed to Vedic deities, whereas a *Brahmana* describes the *yajnas*. There are, in all, five *Samhitas*, eighteen *Brahmanas*, four *Aranyakas* and sixteen Upanishads that are considered as most important.

Rig Veda

It is pre-eminently the worship of nature in its most sublime aspect. The sky that bends over all; the beautiful and blushing dawn that like a busy housewife wakes men from slumber and sends them to work; the gorgeous tropical sun that vivifies the earth; the air that pervades the world; the fire that cheers and frightens; the violent storms that usher in the copious rains which fill the land with plenty were the deities whom the early Hindus loved to extol and worship. Ancient sages like Vashishta and Vishwamitra, who composed these hymns, also fought their wars, ploughed their fields and performed social ceremonies on

The Rig Veda Samhita contained more than 10,000 verses: in the form of over a thousand hymns. As seen above, it expressed the wonder of a people fully awakened to the beauty, grandeur, majesty and mystery of nature. The hymns paint the exquisite glories of the natural world, the preternatural beauty of pre-dawn light and its rosy fingers holding the incandescent blue sky. Some celebrate the welcome cool of evening, the scented breezes of a calm and refreshing night, its basaltic dome studded with shimmering pearls and diamonds. Beauty permeates within them a reflection of Truth. The Rig Veda goes much further in outlining the nature of religion than any other religious texts in use, most of which concentrate on specific aspects of nature's wonder. The Vedic writings, for example, detail a scientific knowledge of the rain cycle that is startlingly true, and project the celebration of life that it has ever created:

Knowledge in Vedic times existed in the form of shrutis *and was transmitted through oral commentaries.*

the banks of the River Saraswati and her tributaries. They wondered about the mystery of the origin of the world most poetically:

> Nor aught nor naught existed; you bright sky
> Was not, nor heaven's broad roof
>   outstretched above;
> What covered all? What sheltered?
>   What concealed?
> Was it the waters' fathomless abyss?
> There was no light of night, no light of day,
> The only One breathed breathless in itself,
> Other than it there nothing since has been.
> Darkness there was, and all at first was veiled
> In gloom profound, an ocean without light ...

> The one who is the life spark of the water,
> Of wood, of things both moving and inert,
> Who has been dwelling even within the stone,
> Immortal Being, He cares for all mankind,
> He who sees all beings at a glance,
> Both separate and united,
> May He be our saviour.

Similarly, *usha* (dawn) is invoked in some of the most beautiful hymns of any ancient nation:

> Beauteous daughter of the sky!
> Hold your ruddy light on high,
> Grant us wealth and grant us day,
> Bring us food and morning's ray.

White-robed goddess of the morning sky,
Bring us light; let night's deep shadows fly...
We gaze upon her as she comes,
The shining daughter of the sky
The mighty darkness she uncovers,
And light she makes, the pleasant one that we see...

Yajur Veda

It is a compilation of mantras and methods that the priests may use while performing Vedic rituals and sacrifices *(yajna)*. Containing a total of 3,988 verses, it is divided into *Krishna* (dark) *Yajur* and *Shukla* (light) *Yajur*, ascribed to Guru Vaisampayana and his feuding pupil Yajnavalka, respectively.

Sama Veda

It is a collection of 1,540 verses set to music by the Vedic priests for chanting during rituals. The use of music in these rituals in metrical chants is considered sanctifying.

Holy bath at River Ganga during tarpan.

Atharva Veda

It is a unique collection of 5,977 verses, it was used to satisfy the daily needs of the common man. This included verses deemed necessary for success in agriculture, trade, progeny, health and general welfare. There were also verses designed to assist in procuring medicine and fighting one's enemy. The Ayurvedic system of medicine, based on the use of herbs for treatment of diseases, has its roots in this Veda.

Upanishads

Occurring at the end of the Vedas (Vedanta), they are crème de la crème of the Vedas, addressing themselves to such quintessential questions as: Where and how does God exist? How are man and the universe related to God? How and why should one try to realise God? What happens when one realises God? Together, the Vedas, the Brahmanas and the Upanishads constitute *shrutis* (what is heard) and are the orally transmitted wisdom of the Hindus. Composed earlier than 700 BC, their basic tenet is that the essence of all beings – from a blade of grass to the perfect human being is the Divine Spirit: Brahman.

Sage Badarayana (around 500 BC) organised the Upanishads into Brahma Sutras or Vedanta Sutras, a compendium of terse aphorisms. This was an attempt to form a cohesive and consistent philosophy out of a variety of ideas expressed in the Upanishads, later giving rise to three major commentaries on the Brahma Sutras: *Dvaita* (Dualism) by Madhava; *Vishishta Advaita* (Qualified Non-Dualism) by Ramanuja; and *Advaita* (Non-Dualism) by Samkara.

Free from theology and dogma, the Upanishads remain the primary source of inspiration and guidance for Hindus and non-Hindus alike, having influenced many Western thinkers like von Goethe, Arthur Schopenhauer and Ralph Waldo Emerson.

The philosophical questions, mentioned in the Upanishads, span the purpose of all lives; origin of the universe; perception of time, space and matter; as well as concepts of Atman, Brahman, *maya*, immortality, rebirth, karma and the material framework. In a nutshell, the Upanishads offer to the world at large the supreme achievement of the awakened and illumined Hindu life. Out of the surviving 108 Upanishads, the following are the principal ones: *Isa, Katha, Prasna, Mundaka, Mandukya, Chandogya, Brihadaranyaka, Taittiriya, Aitareya, Svetasvatara, Kaivalya* and *Maitri.* Their nomenclature as the Vedanta is both because chronologically they come at the end of the Vedas and because philosophically they represent the noblest upshot, the highest watermark of the Vedic civilisation.

Literally, Upanishad also means sitting nearby, implying the dialogue between the guru and the disciples clustering around him in the Indian tradition. Containing the quintessence of *Brahma Vidya* (Knowledge of the Brahman), the Upanishads declare that Brahman is *satchitananda* (the true, the soul and the joy) in its nature, being both the *upadana karana* (material cause) and the *nimitta karana* (efficient cause) of the universe. They declare that karma gives us only perishable fruits and *jnana* can lead to immortality.

Unlike the monotheism of Semitic religions of the West and Islam, which recognise god and creator as distinct from the created beings, the monotheism of the Upanishads treats God as the Universal Being from whom all things have emanated, are a part of Him, and will mingle in Him, and have no separate existence. Taught by Yajnavalkya to his erudite wife Maitreyi and followed by the Hindu religion ever since, this has been the core idea taught in the Upanishads in a hundred similes, well-spun stories and beautiful legends, imparting to the Upanishads their value in the world literature. Here is a gem:

> He is my self within the heart, smaller than a corn of rice, smaller than a mustard seed, smaller than a canary seed, even the kernel of a canary seed. He is also my self within the heart, greater than the sky, greater that the heaven, greater than the sum total of these worlds.

Since the Upanishads intimate that there is a Reality underlying all life that rituals cannot reach, they go beyond philosophy to aim at what can be realised. To that extent, their fervent desire to know is the primary motivation behind all science. While the roots of this scientific spirit were planted in the Vedas, the forest civilisation of the Upanishads took a turn unparalleled in the history of science by focussing on the medium of knowledge—the mind. The self is Brahman, the central discovery of the Upanishads, from which are culled the following nuggets:

- **Ishavashya Upanishad:** *Soham Asmi –* I am That
- **Chandogya Upanishad:** *Tat Tvam Asi –* You are That
- **Aitareya Upanishad:** *Prajnanam Brahman –* Consciousness is Brahman
- **Mandukya Upanishad:** *Ayam Atma Brahman –* This Self is Brahman
- **Brihadaranyaka Upanishad:** *Aham Brahmasmi –* I am Brahman

Here is this Upanishad's most exalted prayer

> From the unreal lead me to the Real,
> From darkness lead me to Light,
> From death lead me to Immortality.

and the duality from *Ishavashya Upanishad*

> It moves, it moves not,
> It is far, and it is near,
> It is within all this,
> And it is beyond all this.

echoing Heisenberg's Principle of Uncertainty within the reality of atomic physics.

Katha Upanishad
It lays down a simple cause–and–effect process between the matter and the spirit or the soul as revealed by the following couplet: 'Like corn the mortal decays and like corn is he born again.' All living beings are held subject to this transmigration process, since they began their journey of evolution in life.

Svetasvatara Upanishad
It questions the ultimate enigma: What is the cause of the universe? Whence are we born? Why do we live?

Where is our final rest? Under whose command are we subject to happiness and misery?

Puranas

There are thirty-six Puranas and five principal Tantras, which continue to be a major source of Hindu mythology. Still revered and read all over India, they are open to all castes. Composed later than the epics of the Ramayana and the Mahabharata, the Puranas exalt a particular god in each. With the Trinity of Brahma–Vishnu–Shiva beginning from the Puranic age, they fall into three major groups: *Brahma, Brahmanda, Brahmavaivarta, Markandeya, Bhavishya* and *Vamana Purana*s in praise of Brahma; *Vishnu, Bhagavata, Naradiya, Garuda, Padma, Matsya, Kurma* and *Varaha Purana*s relating to Vishnu; and *Shiva, Linga, Skanda, Agni* and *Vayu Purana*s chiefly about Shiva.

Veda Vyasa, a revered and immortal entity who had contributed profoundly towards Vedic literature, was deemed the composer and arranger of the eighteen Maha Puranas (major ones), comprising some 400,000 *shloka*s (verses). Veda Vyasa is believed to be. Obviously, there were different hands for such stupendous tomes written at different times, with the basic topics as: creation of the universe, destruction and recreation of the world; genealogy of gods and patriarchs; reign of the fourteen Manus (world-teachers); and history of the monarchs of the Surya and Chandra *vamsha*s (solar and lunar dynasties). The eighteen Maha Puranas are discussed below.

Facing Page: Lord Krishna, symbolising righteousness, plays the cardinal role in spearheading the victory of good over evil.

Agni Purana

Containing 11,450 verses, it is a revelation by Agni in specific rituals, description of the cosmos and the royal art of warfare.

Bhagavata Purana

One of the best known Maha Puranas and probably composed in South India, it has 18,000 verses covering, inter alias, the story of Krishna, origin of the *Ras Lila* and philosophy of *Bhagavata Dharma*.

Bhavishya Purana

Also known as the 'Purana of the future', it has 212 chapters and contains legends of the sun, serpent and fire gods, apart from some historical events, added over time as predictions.

Brahma Purana or Adi Purana

It is known as the first 'old text'. It has 13,800 verses. The bulk narrates the Krishna legend and the rest is devoted to the worship of sun and to Ganesha.

Brahmanda Purana

It is a western Indian work of the ninth century and comprises 12,000 verses. It describes the creation myth: the original cosmic egg yielding all life and the continental islands, and legends related to Parasurama, Rama and Krishna, incarnations of Vishnu.

Brahmavaivarta Purana

It is a Vaishnavite work of the sixteenth century with 10,000 verses. It is esteemed by the Gaudiya, Vallabha and Radhavallabha cults, deifying Radha: Krishna's early love.

Trimurti, the Trinity of Brahma–Vishnu–Mahesh, the Creator, Preserver and Destroyer.

and Krishna, and eulogising Vedic deities like Rudra and Agni. In particular, it narrates the legend of Harishchandra, stressing how karma and its potential can endow men with powers that even the gods do not possess.

Matsya Purana

It contains some 14,000 verses and is one of the first Puranas dating back to the first century. It narrates the story of the first incarnation of Vishnu to save mankind.

Narada Purana

It contains 18,100 verses. It stresses the worship of Vishnu and describes the importance of holy places like Pushkar, Vrindavan, Kurukshetra, Mathura, Badridham, Rameshwaram and Puri.

Padma Purana

It is another popular Vaishnavite Purana, composed in the fourth century (expanded in the sixteenth century) and contains 48,500 verses. It stresses the importance of the worship of Vishnu. Themes of *Abhijnana Shakuntalam* by Kalidasa and *Uttara Rama Charita* by Bhavabhuti were drawn from here.

Skanda Purana

It is the longest of the Puranas and authorship authentically ascribed to Veda Vyasa. It has 81,000 verses and is dedicated to Kartikeya, the son of Shiva and Parvati.

Varaha Purana

It was composed in both prose and verse forms around the tenth century. It narrates the story of

Garuda Purana

It belongs to the tenth century and comprises 8,800 verses. It refers to Garuda (the mythical eagle), as the mount of Vishnu and covers, inter alias, the after-life of deceased family members.

Linga Purana

It was written around the eighth century and has 11,000 verses. It details the significance of the phallic worship of Shiva.

Markandeya Purana

It was composed during the third century. It contains 1,000 verses telling the stories of Rama the incarnation of Vishnu as Varaha (boar) in the elaborate backdrop of Mathura's geography.

Vayu Purana

It is of ancient origin. It contains 24,000 verses, with long descriptions of the Narmada region and the countryside of Malwa, covering details of sacrifices and meaning of dreams and omens.

Vishnu Purana

It is another popular Purana of great antiquity (second century BC) with 6,000 verses. It details out the historically important royalty as well as the Krishna story.

Vamana Purana

It was composed in North India in the seventh century. It delineates the story of the incarnation of Vishnu as Vamana (dwarf), as well as episodes from the Shaiva mythlogy. *Kumara Sambhavam* by Kalidasa was influenced by these legends.

Besides the above-mentioned Puranas, there are sixteen other literary works, called Grihya Sutras (source books of ceremonies and rituals) which were composed between seventh century BC and second century AD. They include *Shankhayana, Bodhayana* and *Jaiminiya,* among others. Together with the Puranas, this enormously rich literary heritage provides a wealth of details of the prevalent mythology, proto-history, history (often surprisingly accurate, as in the *Brahmanda* and *Vishnu Purana*s), geography and cultural geography, apart from offering insight into the Hindu society and psyche.

The mythology of the encyclopaedic Puranas had begun in the pre-Christian era and largely

Sage Valmiki teaching Ramayana to Lava-Kusha, the twin sons of Rama and Sita, who grew up in the Sage's hermitage.

represents the rewriting and standardising of popular traditions associated with the most powerful gods of Hinduism: Shiva and Vishnu. The eighteen Maha Puranas, mentioned above, evolved contemporaneously with Hindu temple art and contain much technical details relating to iconography and sacred architecture. They also describe the various kinds of temple worship and mentions the names of the *tirthas* or places considered as holy by different sects. To popular Hinduism, these massive texts have on one hand, become the sectarian Bibles, and on the other, the verbal recitations of the standard versions of

the myths described in them always attract large audiences of pilgrims and devotees. No wonder, this literary heritage is very much alive still.

The Epics

Pre-dating the Puranas, the creative advances in religion, which followed the Vedic period, are recorded in the Sanskrit epics, the Ramayana and Mahabharata. Of the epics, the Ramayana (around 2300–2000 BC) contains seven *kanda*s (branches) with a total of nearly 24,000 verses and the Mahabharata (around 1400–1000 BC) – the longest poetical work in the world – has eighteen *parva*s (books) with nearly 100,000 verses. Out of these two enormous agglomerations of myths and legends (with perhaps a substantial kernel of the then history), the Ramayana describes the exploits of Rama against the mighty king Ravana and the Mahabharata narrates the epic story of internecine struggle between the Kaurava and Pandava cousins, with Krishna helping the latter.

While the epic stories are well known to all, they depict, in substance, the Hindu ages when the gods manifested themselves on earth and man could stand up to them: without the need for intermediary images in stone and metal. The religious and political nostalgia for this remote age is visible everywhere in the later secular literature and drama.

Ramayana

It is ascribed to Sage Valmiki. The epic tends to describe the proto-history of the Aryan consolidation

Facing page: *The central characters of the Ramayana: Rama, Lakshmana, Sita and Hanumana.*

of the country from north to south: taking all possible help from the non-Aryans. In the legends, there seems a severe gradation among the non-Aryans, described often in animal forms and the story stretches over the ultimate overruling of the furthest non-Aryans – termed *rakshasas* (demons) – having a surprisingly advanced civilisation. Two other striking features are: one, the benevolence of the gods shared fairly equitably between Rama – as *Maryada Purushottama* (the noblest of men) – and the Shiva-worshipper, demon-king Ravana; and two, the general ambivalence between the virtuous and the vicious, with the 'bad' never painted as completely 'evil', but as a 'soul gone astray', with testing and redemption available round the corner.

The principal morals of the Ramayana spins around the web of karma, as the consequences of past deeds, and the sacrifice of freedom for the sake of duty and honour are the essential purposes of life. In Hindu society, this manifests itself as a set of principles governing behaviour and adherence to family bonds.

In depicting scenes of intimate affection and expressing feelings and emotions that belong to the human race in all times and places, the epic poetry stands unrivalled, even in comparison to the Greek epics. Many poetic passages, besides throwing light on the high ideals of purity and happiness of domestic life in ancient India, describe the ability of the Indian woman to perform her sacred and social duties. There are indications in the epic of a higher degree of civilisation than perhaps the Homeric poems. The battlefields of the Ramayana are not made of barbarously wanton cruelties; in fact, the description of Ayodhya and Lanka imply greater luxury and refinement than those of Sparta and Troy. Rama is the archetype of a perfect husband, son and brother. Sita also rises in character much above Helen and even above Penelope, both in the sublime devotion and loyalty to her husband, and her indomitable patience and endurance under suffering and temptation. The whole tone of the Ramayana is arguably above that of the Iliad.

The Ramayana means, in essence, Rama's travels. Since the time of Valmiki, many Indian poets have made their translations and adaptations of the epic, which include Kamba in Tamil, Tulsidas in Hindi, Krittibas Ojha in Bengali and Sarala in Oriya, apart from the translations in other languages like Kashmiri, Kannada, Telugu and Malayalam. True to its name, it migrated across Southeast Asia (Suvarna Bhumi), to countries like Thailand and Indonesia, each of who have their own Ramayana literary traditions and have made it a part of their culture. In Thailand, the Ramayana dance drama is the national

A scene from the Mahabharata depicting the battle of Kurukshetra, fought between the Kauravas and the Pandavas and culminating into the victory of dharma *over* adharma.

dance: an inheritance of the country's ancient Hindu past, and the Thai king traditionally models himself on Rama. Indonesia is famous for its shadow puppet (Wayang Purwa) and rod puppet (Wayang Golek) theatre depicting the Ramayana. Its enormously large orb of influence in India and abroad, with the surprising prevalence in the Buddhist Southeast Asia and the Islamic belts of Java and elsewhere, is indeed unparalleled in the literary annals of any other epic.

Mahabharata

It is supposedly ascribed to Veda Vyasa. The eradication of the non-Aryan influence is no longer the issue and it is a proto-history of alignments as well as alienations among the fairly stable royal dynasties under their powerful heads. In the pan-Indian efforts at expansion and consolidation of influence, there are many subterranean issues like the role of the subservient women, prevalence of deceit in power games and occasionally great show of virtuous values and Krishna's supreme role as the surrogate centre of power.

As one of the greatest literary works of the world, the Mahabharata is unique in various ways: for the deepest philosophical truths, for the wide range of human life covered by the ethics and for the high spiritual stimulus provided throughout the epic. While ostensibly it is the story of a devastating war between two rival sections of a dynasty, it is in reality the tale of evolution of all life: a treatise on cosmology, a code of universal ethics, and a history of human race in its most general sense.

All life is rooted in the One Life: the deities, sages, men, beasts, flowers, rocks: everything in

Veda Vyas is believed to be the composer of Mahabharata.

the manifested universe have evolved in and from that One Life. There is a Great Plan in the mind of God (*Ishwara Sankalpa*) and everything that was, that is and that shall be, happens according to that Plan. In sharp contrast to existential philosophy, human free will is part of that Plan.

The Mahabharata is a treasure house on ancient India: with history, statecraft, religion and mythology woven into a rich and glorious fabric. The massive epic describes, in essence, the ideal polity, culture and religion, and may be termed as the 'Epic of Society and State', outlining the victory of righteousness. There is scarcely any human situation that it leaves untouched, and covers almost all contingencies that mankind could experience till recently. Unlike the Ramayana, which deals with the ideal types, the Mahabharata is so intensely human that it still has a special resonance in the Indian heart. It is a text that reveals deeper meanings as one's life unfolds, and a superlative guide to humans trying to work out their entire lifespan, with its hold on the imagination showing little sign of diminishing. In the finale of the epic, Veda Vyasa writes:

> Dharma is eternal; life, its joys and sorrows are not. Do not give away the eternal for the temporal values of life. ... Do not do to others what you do not wish / done to yourself; and wish for others too / what you desire and long for, for yourself – This the whole of Dharma – heed it well.

Smritis and Shrutis

Smritis (what is remembered) form the large part of the sacred literature of the Hindus and remain valid, unless contradicted by the *shrutis* (what is heard). They consist mainly of the two epics, the eighteen Maha Puranas, the Dharma Shastras (treatises of religious religions law), the Smartha Sutras (sacramental treatises), the six Vedangas (limbs of the Vedas) and the Niti Shastras (ethical treatises). However, treatises on the six *darshanas* (philosophies) stand as a class apart, considered neither *shrutis* nor *smritis*.

Incidentally, the Indian art of writing seems very old, with the *Rig Veda* and *Yajur Veda* containing sacred references to write, draw and form letters (*akshara*, meaning what cannot be obliterated). The two major scripts were *Brahmi* (written from left to right) and *Kharoshthi* (written from right to left). Palm leaf, birch, handmade paper, cloth, wooden slabs, silk and leather were all used as writing material, and permanent writings were carved on stones, bricks, gold, silver, copper, brass and iron plates.

Bhagavad Gita

Read and recited daily by millions in India over the centuries, the Bhagavad Gita has been the source of inspiration to individuals, to seekers of enlightenment and peace, and to leaders of great social and political movements. Forming a part of the epic Mahabharata, its eighteen chapters sing perhaps the most beautiful paeans of philosophy possible in any language. The contents are brought out in the form of a dialogue: between Krishna and Arjuna, located in the battlefield, where Arjuna has the unenviable task of fighting his cousins, nephews, family-elders, teachers and friends. Metaphorically, the battlefield is life itself, where we are constantly engaged in a struggle, both within and without. An excellent work on religion and ethics, the Bhagavad Gita declares that God dwelling in the heart of all beings moves them to action. It proclaims that there are many paths (Yogas) of reaching the spiritual goal of life and that one should never disturb the faith of others, whose understanding is poor. The different ways of knowing God are broadly: Jnana Yoga – the way of wisdom; Bhakti Yoga – the way of love of god; Karma Yoga – the way of selfless action; and Raja Yoga – the way of meditation.

Broadly, the message of the Bhagavad Gita to modern man can be summarised through the following aphorisms:

- *Gita is not only a philosophy, but a code of conduct for man.* Hence, the text is applicable

- to varying temperaments, vocations and levels of development.
- *There is unity in life as well as consequent interdependence of everything in the world.* The Gita emphasises on the imminence of God, making the wise to look beyond the veil of what is deceptive and illusionary, for the common basis of all beings.
- *Dedicated action does not bind, but frees the man.* The Gita severely condemns the attitude of escapism stating: 'nor can anyone, even for an instant, remain action-less'.

Sangam poets lived in renunciation as monks.

- *Gita is a gospel of hope and optimism.* Though men are weak and full of faults, they all reach the goal, since men are divine in essence. Their divinity is only veiled: rend the veil and the inner divinity reveals itself.
- *Divine manifestations come to restore righteousness.* This happens when humans are trampled under the foot, by their selfishness and perversity.

Tamil Texts

In the early part of the first millennium, Tamil literature was highly developed. Great poetry from the then prevalent Sangam literature (100 BC–AD 500) comprised eight anthologies of *Ahinanuru* and *Pattupatu* with splendidly written emotional poems, revealing the depths of poetic feelings. Besides, Sangam literature, *Thirukkural* is an exquisite poetic work of 1,330 verses (comprising couplets and quartets) on the ethics and *dharma* to be followed by both family men and saints. Composed by the great Tamil writer, Thiruvaluvar, who came from a family of weavers in Tanjavur, this magnum opus has three parts: *arabppal* (on *dharma*); *poorotpal* (on instructions for the kings); and *inbathupal* (on pleasures of life).

By the second century AD, five epics appeared in the South, not necessarily at the same time, but known together as the 'Tamil Quintets': *Silppadikaram, Mani Mekhalai, Jeevaka Chintamani, Kundalakeshi* and *Valayapathi*. Two remarkable facts about them are that, first, their authors were all monks, probably Buddhist or Jain. One wonders whether renunciation of domestic life provided the needed distancing to write about the latter! Second, all the five works were related to women's jewellery, anklets on the feet; waist bands; necklaces with gems; ear rings; and arm bangles, respectively!

Silappadikaram

It is by far the most well-known epic (second century AD) written by Ilango Adigal. Its tale is rooted in the ordinary lives of the people from the Pandyan kingdom and provides a rich cultural knowledge: irreplaceably valuable in understanding ancient and modern South Indian thinking.

Its unique importance lies in several factors: one, the story is a cogent history of the Chera, Chola and Pandiya culture; two, it depicts the deeds of an ordinary family woman, rather that the heroic deeds of kings; three, it has a memorial erected for a virtuous woman, and not for kings and monarchs; four, it is different from the prevailing emotion-laden Sangam poetry; five, its author's secular character is never doubted, although he is a Jain monk; and six, it offers glimpses of rare literary beauty. Most of all, it has a mine of information on the prevalent music and dance quoted from *Nrithyanannul* (also cited in Malayalam literature), a compendium on performing arts perhaps of the same stature as Bharata's *Natya Shastra* and of the same antiquity (second century AD).

The epic has been translated and adopted in many different languages, especially in the Kannada dramatic oeuvre by Shiva Prakash: *Madhura Kande, Madhavi* and *Matruka*. In the story, the 'eternal triangle' – among the businessman Kovalan, his faithful wife Kannagi and the beauteous danseuse Madhavi – results in the former getting indicted and executed on the false charge of stealing the queen's anklet (hence the name) and the enraged Kannagi setting fire to the city of Tanjavur, later to be elevated as a folk-goddess.

The only other parallel of such elevation to godhood from the pages of literature is 'Radha' of Jayadeva's *Gita Govinda*: by the Telugu poet Nimbarka in the sixteenth century in Vrindavana, to be deified as 'Radha-Krishna' everywhere since.

Mani Mekhalai

It was authored by Seethalai Sathanar. This epic takes off from Madhavi's daughter turning away from dance to sainthood and expressly promoting Buddhist philosophy, with an *akshaya patra* (endless food pot) to counter hunger.

Jeevaka Chintamani

It was authored by Chiru Thakkathevar. It has been compared to the Iliad and Odyssey. Its 3,000 love poems on the libidinous king Jeevaka, who became a saint later, juxtapose the instability of youth with wealth and body. It is also known as a 'book of marriage'.

Kundalakesi

It was authored by Natha Kuthannar. It is sourced from *Vaisya Purana*, a minor Purana prevalent in the South. No proper text is available, except that it establishes Buddhist philosophy, among others.

Valayapathi

It is also sourced from *Vaisya Purana,* its authorship is unknown. No proper text is available besides explaining Jaina philosophy. The devotional movement had struck root in the South by the seventh century, giving rise to the genre of Bhakti poetry by Alvars, who composed a very large number of verses *(prabandham),* with available commentaries. This tradition began in the lifetime of Ramanuja with works like *Arayirappatu* (literally, 6,000 *shloka*s).

These Vaishnavite poets were worshippers of Venkatesha. Among the top twelve – Kulasekhara Alvar, a king; Tiruppana Alvar, a member of the depressed class; Tirumangai Alvar, belonging to the so-called criminal tribe; and the peasant-poet Namma Alvar whose *Thiru Vayamoli* was the most important work of *Prabandham,* with five old commentaries totalling to the size of the Mahabharata: with some 87,000 *pasurams* (songs). The greatest Alvar poetess was Andaal, regarded (though born earlier) as Mira of the South, who wrote thirty songs called *Thiruppavai,* still sung by millions of people, including children's choir groups. *Nalayira Divya Prabandham* exists as an anthology by twelve major Alvar poets.

Another tradition around the ninth–tenth century was *thevaram,* the song cycle contributed by Nayanars, the Shaivite poets. Their major saint-poets were: Manikka Vachagar, Karaikkal Ammaiyur, Thirujnana Sambandar and Sundaramurthy, apart from the poetess Avviyar. The tales and legends of Thevaram poets are extant in the inner precinct paintings of the Brihadishwara Temple, as are Andaal's songs from *Thiruppavai*—imbued with the bridal mysticism—still sung in the Srivillipuhur Temple: in the month of *Marga Sirsa* (15 December–15 January). The reformist Shaivite movement of Basava (twelfth century) led to the emergence of a great lyrical–philosophical tradition especially in Karnataka.

The seat for a holy book is considered as sacred as the book itself.

Devotional Tapestry

Bhakti poetry indeed permeated India between seventh–nineteenth centuries and worked at two levels. Either, they signalled surrender of self to a personal god, as evident in Thyagaraja's compositions, or they decried caste, untouchability and social hierarchy through satirical, wrathful or melancholy lyrics, like Kabir's outpourings. Mostly hailing from the lower strata of society, they used simple language to inspire the common man to militate against Brahmanism.

Two streams of Bhakti poetry that emerged were either *nirguna* (sans any Godhead) or *saguna* (invoking a Godhead). *Nirguna* verses, influenced by Buddhism, were *prem-margi* (seeking love) or *jnan-margi* (seeking knowledge). In contrast, *saguna* verses branched into *Rama-bhakti* (devotion to Rama) or *Krishna-bhakti* (devotion to Krishna). These streams added rich poetic legacy to literature,

Statue of Buddha, Sarnath School of Art. Buddhism influenced the Bhakti movement to a great extent.

beginning with Gorakhnath and espoused by Nanak, Dadu, Namdev, Tukaram, Kabir and many others, often forging linkages with Sufism. On the whole, Bhakti poets provided a lot of inner strength to the Indian people and persuaded them to adopt non-material thinking, an enduring spiritual inheritance to the masses and sustained survival against adversity.

Sanskrit Texts

The efflorescence of Sanskrit literature – in poetry, prose, drama and numerous other manifestations – has been a matter of highest creativity. On the whole, the literary creativity of the Vedas and Upanishads continued an unabated flow along the millennia and flowered into magnificent epics, enticing fiction, great parables and some exquisite poetry and drama. This vitality – beginning with religious search for knowledge and culminating into creative literature in eighteen well-developed languages drawing from the same fountainheads – is an astounding unbroken tradition of an ancient civilisation. The dating of ancient Indian literary masters, as much as the events and other figures of importance, is not an easy process, and often results in numerous theories (such as, who mentioned whom as a predecessor, whose writings reveal what contemporary landscape, etc.). Within that framework, the following chronology is a glimpse of India's enormously rich literary heritage.

Pre-Christian Millennium

- **Panini** composed one of the oldest, well-known grammar *Ashtadhyayi* (eight chapters), containing 3,996 *sutras* (aphorisms). A linguistic phenomenon, he describes the language accurately without any preconceived theory.

- **Kautilya** wrote *Arthashastra* catering to the pragmatic sides of commerce, politics and diplomacy. It is comparable to the much later works of Machiavelli.
- **Ashvaghosha** composed *Buddha Charita* (biography of the Buddha) and *Saundara Ananda* (a renowned drama) both of which are still available. Fragments of one of his plays called, *Sariputra Prakarana*, have been found in Central Asia.

Turn of the Christian Millennium

The period between the first and second century AD may be considered as the 'Golden Century', of India, perhaps even richer than the Greek 'Golden Century' of the fifth century BC. With comparative social peace, increasing economic prosperity and cultural unity, and wider contacts abroad, this century envisions enhanced trade (both internally and overseas) and more circulation of culture (not only within the country, but also to Southeast Asia, the Far East and the Mediterranean).

By the middle of the first century, Buddhism has reached China and by the end of the century, the Roman Emperor has received an Indian mission in Europe. Internally, mercantile and professional guilds have become wealthy and begin giving patronage to learning and the arts. This is not merely the scholarly times of Bhasa and Bharata, and of Ilango Adigal and Seethalai Sathanar, but also the time of the physician Charaka (author of the astonishingly detailed *Charaka Samhita*); the age of the flourishing of Gandhara art – extending

Kalidasa, a renowned poet and dramatist of Sanskrit literature.

up to Mathura and the beauteous sculptures of the nascent Odissi form on the Rajarani Temple in Bhuvaneswar, apart from the cave temple of Karle and the earliest ones of Ajanta; and the period when the Code of Manu assumed its final form.

- **Bhasa** composed thirteen highly evolved plays – delineating human psychology and staging violence. Though these were physically untracable and were earlier known only by

Naga deities, Mahabalipuram (sixth to eighth centuries), Tamil Nadu: animals were worshipped as deities from Vedic times.

hearsay they were re-discovered fortuitously in palm-leaf manuscripts in 1909. One of the greatest playwrights of all times, Bhasa adopted from the Mahabharata six plays: *Madhyama Vyayoga* (The Middle One, about the confusion around Bhima, the middle Pandava); *Pancha Ratram* (Five Nights, about the last few days of the Pandavas in disguise); *Duta Vakyam* (The Envoy, about Krishna's mission as plenipotentiary); *Duta Ghatotkacham* (The Message, about an imagined visit of Ghatotkach to the Kaurava camp); *Karnabharam* (Karna's Burden, about his unburdening of soul to Shalya); and the only tragedy in Sanskrit, *Urubhangam* (The Shattered Thigh, about Duryodhan's death and lamentation).

The remaining seven plays are: *Abhiseka, Pratima, Balacharita, Swapna Vasavdatta, Pratijna Yaugandharayana, Charudatta* and *Avimaraka*. While the first two plays are drawn from the Ramayana, the third one is from the Krishna stories of the *Hari Vamsa* and the last four are from other stories prevalent at that time.

- **Bharata** authored *Natya Shastra,* the oldest work of Indian literary criticism, and a comprehensive compendium on *nritta* (abstract dance postures), *nritya* (interpretative dance) and *natya* (theatrical action) in terms which are amazingly detailed and scientific, embracing both *margi* (classical) and *desi* (regional) kinds of performance. On theatre, the *Natya Shastra* suggests the dimensions of theatre halls, categorises ten types of dramatic performances and covers all aspects of theatrical art.

- **Amarasinha** authored the oldest and the most comprehensive Sanskrit thesaurus, *Amara Kosha,* full of short parables.
- **Sudraka** authored *Mrichchakatika* (the Clay Cart), a famous social drama about the Brahmin Charudatta and the courtesan Vasantasena.
- **Kalidasa** was a renowned poet and dramatist in Sanskrit literature. He penned four poetic works: *Ritu Samharam* (the Gathering of the Seasons, an ode to all six Indian seasons); *Kumara Sambhavam* (the Birth of Kartikeya, the son of Shiva and Parvati); *Raghuvamsam* (about the Raghu Dynasty); and the most celebrated *Meghadutam* (the Cloud Messenger, the banished Yaksha's message to his far-away beloved). His three plays are the well-known *Abhijnanam Shakuntalam* (the love-affair, desertion and eventual recognition of the hermit-girl Shakuntala); *Vikramorvashiam* (the love story of the mortal king Pururaba and the celestial nymph Urvashi, referred to in the *Rig Veda*); and *Malavikagnimitram* (the love of a king for his court-dancer).
- **Vishakhadatta** wrote the enduring classic *Mudra Rakshasa* (the Minister's Signet Ring, on Chanakya's clever ploy to win over Rakshasa, the fallen minister of the Nandas).
- **Vatsyayana** wrote *Kama Sutra,* a unique work in seven chapters on the erotic arts, is regarded as the world's greatest classic on the subject.

Sixth Century to Tenth Century

- **Banabhatta** was a master of Sanskrit prose. He authored *Kadambari* (a romantic tale) and *Harsha Charita* (a biography of King Harshavardhana).

- **Bharavi** authored the epic *Kirata Arjuniyam,* in eighteen cantos, based on the Shiva–Arjuna encounter from the Mahabharata.
- **Bhartrihari** was a highly accomplished poet and composer. He wrote *Shringara Shataka* (an erotic filigree carved for a king, a gifted poet and a jilted lover, alongside human emotions of love and rejection), *Niti Shataka* (a book of manners for a ruler and duty towards his subjects, value of education, pitfalls of greed and lust, and rewards of good deeds) and *Vairagya Shataka* (on asceticism, self-discovery and importance of meditation and renunciation), each in poems of a hundred stanzas.
- **Dandin** wrote *Dashakumara Charita* (Tales of Ten Princes) and *Simhasana Dwatrinshika* which were prose collections of exciting adventures and parables on King Vikramaditya's mythical throne of thirty two puppets. These were followed by *Vetala Pancha Vinshati* (twenty-five tales told by the Hovering Spirit), comprising delightful anecdotes.
- **Somadeva** wrote *Katha Sarit Sagara* (An Ocean of Stories), in easy, elegant verse, using a body of 350 folktales and folklore.
- **Bhavabhuti** was one of the best-known playwright after Kalidasa. He wrote *Mahavira Charita* (on the story of Ramayana till Rama's return to Ayodhya); *Uttara Rama Charita* (the story from the banishment of the pregnant queen Sita to her ultimate disappearance underground); and *Malati Madhava* (story of a couple of young Buddhist monks, planned to be married off).
- **Sriharsha** was also known as the poet king of Thaneswar. He wrote two plays: *Ratnavali* (love

story of princess Vasavadatta) and *Naganada* (a symbolic story of snakes, for uniting the Hindus and Buddhists).

- **Patanjali** was a renowned literary figure. His *Mahabhashya* is an erudite critique of Panini's seminal work on Sanskrit grammar.

Eleventh Century Onwards

- **Vishnu Sharman** wrote *Panchatantra* (Five Treatises) to impart moral instructions through simple stories about animals and men, apparently to educate recalcitrant princes, placed under his charge.
- **Narayana** wrote *Hitopodesha,* a book meant for children and based on the *Panchatantra.*
- **Jayadeva** wrote the unique dance text *Gita Govinda* in exquisite lyrical cadences on the love, separation and eventual union of Krishna and Radha. It fostered innumerable commentaries all over India and Nepal, giving rise to illumined manuscripts. It inspired countless Rajasthani, Pahadi and Deccani miniature paintings. Its text was used at the Manipur, Orissa and Kerala temples. All the classical dance styles of India use its text for *nritya* (interpretative dance).

Manuscripts

As an ancient literary civilisation – with a literary tradition much longer than most, stretching thousands of years – India holds manuscripts in a variety of locations: temples, monasteries, archives and private homes. Arguably the most diverse literary tradition in the world, the manuscripts run into some five million, with myriad languages, scripts, themes, materials and aesthetic aspects: with a vast reservoir of knowledge and memory, dating back to the earliest of times.

To round up this literary survey, six special points need to be made. First, the above account does not cover the Pali and Prakrit texts. Pali was a predominant language in the early millennium and primarily used for Buddhist canonical writing, comprising the *Tripitaka* (Three Baskets). The non-canonical works are commentaries, historical writing and technical treatises, besides epigraphical literature. The second most important language was Prakrit, later termed *apabhramsa* (modified derivation), having both canonical and non-canonical works. While the former are all Jaina treatises, the latter comprise narrative, lyrical and dialectic poetry; short stories; dramas; lexicons; geography; cosmogony; astronomy; philosophy; ethics; as well as inscriptions.

Second, Vishnu Sharman's *Panchatantra* and Somadeva's *Katha Sarit Sagar* were crowning achievements of the Hindu culture, with didactic anecdotes, animal stories, fairy tales, novellas, fables and simple parables – composed often as *mahakavya* (epic poetry). They were devoted to the sublimely popular art of storytelling in the medieval India, inspiring much of the Islamic and European literature in later centuries, including the famous *Aesop's Fables*.

Third, the second half of the first millennium also saw the flowering of Sanskrit aestheticians and their work. Much literary criticism, flourished from AD 600 to AD 1600, related to the soul of poetry, role of sound in poetry, figures of speech and oblique poetry, apart from the origin, process and impact of poetry: with choice of words, meanings and undertones as well as the psychological and sociological aspects of the poetic compositions.

Fourth, competent translations of the classics paid handsome dividends in restoring the heritage, and Islam played an important role in this effort. The Mahabharata was translated during the Muslim times. Darah Shukoh, one of the sons of Emperor Shah Jahan translated the Upanishads. In the colonial times, Cole Brooke translated the Vedas and Wilkins the Bhagavad Gita. William Jones translated *Abhijnanam Shakuntalam* and founded the Asiatic Society of Bengal in 1783. It became a centre of excellence for Sanskrit language and literature which came to be known all over within half a century and its range and richness dazzled the world.

Fifth, a rich crop of regional languages—both in the North and the South—originated from Sanskrit and its derivatives like Pali and Prakrit. Each of them today has a large spoken group and an enormously varied literature: ranging from sacred to secular and easily comparable to any major European language. Litterateurs, using these languages, have immensely contributed to the outcrop of poetry, philosophy, fiction, short stories, drama and a host of other literary genres, much of which unmistakably draw inspiration from the hoary source texts of Hinduism.

Sixth and finally, as has been seen, the literary creativity of the Vedas and Upanishads continued in an unabated flow down the millennia and flowered into magnificent epics, enticing fictions, great parables and some of the most exquisite poetry and drama of the world. This vitality – beginning with the religious quest for knowledge and culminating in eighteen well-developed

Manuscripts are the primary source of information for ancient traditions, customs, languages and religion.

national languages – has been drawn from the same fountainheads and is an astounding unbroken tradition of an ancient civilisation.

Chapter Seven

Visual Arts

Visual Arts

The imagination and skills of artists, artisans and architects attained concrete shape and found expression in numerous art forms that represented the gods and their abodes.

Konarak Temple, Orissa: a specimen of exemplary Indian architecture.

The earliest inhabitants of India worshipped and meditated upon the sunrise, the midday sun, the sunset, alongside the natural elements like the sky, fire and earth. The Vedic sages did not conceive of complex icons and their rituals did not go beyond words (mantras) and gestures (*mudras*). The anthropomorphic images emerged only gradually: a virgin to visualise dawn *(usha);* three images of the sun in separate hues; fire as a divine planner; and so on. The angular platforms and arrangements of the sacred pillars and firewood for *yajna* were an intricate, yet aesthetic, process of geometry. Arts began to flourish when the artists, artisans and architects gave concrete shape to their imagination and evolved their skills of design and development to find aesthetic expressions in representing the gods and their abodes.

According to the Vedanta, everything in nature was beautiful. It suggested of an inward harmony in the universe. Both the Vedanta and Samkhya schools allowed derivation of aesthetic enjoyment from nature, and the aim of art was to reduce a mood of detachment to enhance pleasure. The *Aitareya Brahman* highlighted *chhanda* (skill and rhythm) – including regularity, balance, proportion and harmony – as the core of *kala* (art). The concept of art meant literally *Karyesu Kaushalam* (skill in an activity). Art, as *kala* or *shilpa*, was seen as a means to achieve supreme beauty. Beauty could be either metaphysical (including ethical or transcendental beauty), or as experienced in the visual arts (painting, architecture, sculpture, and handicrafts) and poetry (including physical, natural and mental perceptions).

Painting

Pictures, which express emotions through colours were, according to the *Vishnudharmottara Purana,* aimed at displaying mental and physical changes and variations of emotions. Vatsyayana's *Kama Sutra* divided painting under six heads: face and physiognomy; measurement and proportions; authenticity of emotion; outward harmony; recognisable identity; and consistency in the colours used. In ancient India, references are replete that mention places and homes of the nobility decorated with beautiful murals. In the two works of visual aesthetics, *Chitralakshana* gave a detailed description of the art of painting and *Shilparatna* delineated techniques of combining tints, preparing surfaces of the walls and other minute details.

Mural Tradition

- **Ajanta** – The earliest efflorescence of painting in India comprised the magnificent cave paintings here. These mural paintings, spanning a whole millennium: from the third century BC to the seventh century AD: are no doubt based on Buddhist themes, but they also illustrate the entire life of India: princes and princesses in palaces; queens and maids-in-attendance; dancing maidens; load-carriers laden with burdens slung over their shoulders; warriors, beggars, ascetics and monks; peasants and common men in procession; elephants as well as horses: depicted and painted with consummate artistic skill. Some women are shown even in high-heeled shoes, with varied coiffures, and carrying purses! Like Plato, the Ajanta artists equate physical and moral beauty, and undraped women are shown in perfect loveliness, mingling with men.

  The greatness of the Ajanta art lies in its handling of human anatomy with superb decorative sense and a sensuous intuition of form and colour.

  Indeed, there are depictions of the baby at the mother's breast; the child at play; the youth at his pleasures; and the turning away from the domestic hearth. It is in this descent of art to the ordinary people's level that marks the greatest significance of the Ajanta art.

- **Badami –** Remnants of the seventh-century paintings here are a continuation of the Ajanta-type mural painting, together with the eighth-century paintings at Tirunandikkara, Tamil Nadu. The seventh-century Pallava paintings at Sittannavasal also show the grace and simplicity of Ajanta.

- **Ellora –** The eighth-century paintings here, with angular lines, are still remarkable in execution.

- **Brihadishwara** – This Chola temple at Tanjavur (eleventh century) displays, on the inner walls, remarkably detailed stories and legends of the Shaiva saint-poets, in a serially narrative style.
- **Vijayanagaar** – Indian paintings of the fourteenth–fifteenth century such as those found in Lepakshi show higher stylisation and sharper outlines, with an assimilation of the folk idiom.
- **Padmanabhapuram** – The sixteenth -century paintings here reveal a baroque richness of details, though the eighteenth-century Mattanchey prefers a vigorous realism.

Manuscript Illustration

When painting descended from the wall to the palm-leaf and paper in Western India, there emerged a tradition of manuscript illustration. In the manuscripts of Pala period (ninth to twelfth century), the melodic, undulating line of Ajanta finds its reincarnation on a miniature scale.

- **Vasanta Vilas** – There is lyricism depicted on a painted roll of cloth, which carries the irresistibly romantic theme of dalliance in spring.
- **Gita Govinda** – The twenty-four-canto musical poem on the Radha-Krishna dalliance got illustrated in exquisitely illumined manuscripts on palm-leaf, tree-bark, cloth and paper, all over India. Thanks to the immense popularity of the Jayadeva epic, the manuscript illustrations spread like wild fire from east to west, particularly Bengal, Orissa and Assam.

Painting depicting Krishna with Radha and the gopis.

Miniature Art

Miniature painters, depicting similar themes, show influence of Persian portraiture, establishing their openness to absorb outside influences. Nonetheless, the freshness of feeling and colour, acquired by the later Gujarat miniatures, foreshadow the quality of Rajput miniature.

The literary and religious traditions of India began to pour into this mould and took away the mere sensuous elegance that characterised the Persian style.

- **Rajput School** – Songs about the seasons – always a rich strand in the folk heritage – provided themes for the new Rajput style. A feeling for river and meadow, cloud and sky, foliage and flower is reflected in Rajput paintings.

  Though artists of various Rajput schools were certainly trained or worked at the Mughal courts, nature begins to be seen through literary memories. Cranes in flight in the cloud-laden monsoon sky allude to Kalidasa, or, a garland of white lotuses suggest Valmiki, apart from the unmistakable, doe-eyed Kishengarh Radha.

- **Pahadi School** – Apart from the visualisation of the above metaphors, here are the profiles of woman in longing, expectation or sorrow, as had been the tradition of *Nayika* literature. One can see Radha in all these moods in the evocative visualisation of the Pahadi artists.

The Vaishnavite religious movement, which evoked a lyrical fervour – released by the metaphor of God as

Krishna holding Govardhan mountain, a specimen of Orissa painting.

the lover of the human soul – became the undoubted source of inspiration for both these schools.

Architecture

From the period of the Indus Valley Civilisation, Indian architecture has been evolving steadily over the time span of five millennia. The pre-Aryan civilisation developed a material culture comparable to that of the pre-Hellenic Aegean culture: with every house having a bathroom in addition to public baths. While houses made of burnt brick, were double-storeyed, a large, excavated public path was also built of burnt bricks, with an excellent drainage system. The pastoral Aryans inherited and enriched the tradition.

In the *Rig Veda,* there are mention of deities and sovereigns who occupied a '... great palace with a thousand pillars and a thousand gates'. Generally, the Vedic and Brahmanical era held the craftsmen in high esteem, as they were the hewers and builders of the altars on which the priest-kings performed their rites of sacrifices *(yajna).* Also, mention of bungalows, *prasadas* (storeyed palaces) and *harmyas* (storeyed mansions in several rows or blocks) are found in the epics. The Buddhist text *Chullabhagga* states that houses comprised living rooms, retiring rooms, halls with fireplaces, closets and cloisters, halls for exercises, wells and ponds, bathrooms and hot-air baths.

In the course of centuries, India developed a variety of architectural forms. In the Buddhist times, cloisters grew around a central monument that contained the sacred relics and the beautiful

Ellora elephant, bearing evidence of outstanding workmanship.

horseshoe-shaped portal of these *viharas* were successfully adopted in the contemporary styles.

- **Ashokan Pillars** – Thirty in number, they were erected by Ashoka for publishing his edicts in the third century BC. They were monoliths with exceedingly polished surfaces and stood at places of pilgrimage or on highways carrying Buddhist symbols at the top.
- **Ellora** – The rock-cut architecture reached its pinnacle at Ellora (seventh century) where temples of exceptionally-skilled workmanship were carved out of huge monoliths, such as the marvellous Kailasa Temple (as Shiva's shrine), abode of Ravana, ten incarnations of Vishnu and other works of art.

North Indian Temples

Among the few ancient and important temples extant in North India, those at Bhuvaneswar are much valued for their architectural excellence. The very well-carved Lingaraja Temple (tenth century), dedicated to Shiva, is 150-feet high, has a beautiful tapering tower supporting sedentary gryphon and is crowned by a vase-shaped finial *(kalasa)* with Shiva's trident. The famous temple of the Sun-god at Konarak is made of mortar-less blocks of laterite-stone to resemble a juggernaut, a gigantic solar chariot with twelve pairs of wheels drawn by seven spirited horses, held in exquisite equilibrium. The Jagannath Temple, in Orissa, is another architectural marvel. Among the group of a dozen shrines at Khajuraho (tenth century), the largest is the

Konarak Wheel at the Sun Temple in Orissa.

Kanderiya Mahadeva Temple: 116-feet high and with most refined, sensuous sculptures alongside the mystic ones. In Gujarat and western India, there are several magnificent temples now mostly in ruins.

South Indian Temples

In the South, the Dravidians were great builders and their Meenakshi Temple (seventh century) at Madurai, dedicated to Shiva's consort, is the greatest and most famous shrine, with extraordinarily beautiful *gopurams* (gateways): on all four sides. The Brihadishwara Temple in Tanjavur is the finest single creation of the Dravidian *sthapathis* (architects) and craftsmen, along with its nearby shrine at Gangaikundacholapuram, both dedicated to Shiva.

The great Vaishnava Temple (seventeenth century) at Srirangam has a wonderful 'hall of thousand

Hall of thousand pillars, an architectural splendour at Srirangam.

pillars': with 900 carved granite monoliths. The Nataraja Temple (thirteenth century) at Chidambaram has the image of Shiva as a divine dancer. The famous eight seaside pagodas (eighth century) at Mahabalipuram, near Chennai, are masterpieces of chariots hewn out of monolithic granite, carved from outcrops of boulders. The Halebid Temple in Karnataka has two different vestibule sanctums, joined by short corridors. The artistic combination of horizontal and vertical lines, and the play of light and shade are unique, with no two canopies of the temple being alike.

Sculpture

According to *Shukra Niti*: 'Images of the gods yield happiness and lead to heaven; but those of men ... yield grief.' While episodes of the Buddha and his life were the starting points in figurative architecture of the Gandhara period (first century AD), the Hindu sculptors aimed at achieving perfection in depicting in stone the kinesthetic movement. From the terracotta of the Indus Valley civilisation to the expressionistic work of today, Indian sculpture has seen a magnificent revolution: with almost every century recording a fresh stylistic development and each region modulating in subtle ways the basic idiom of its time.

The notable Hindu sculpture of early India was from the Mathura School: with many secular figures of richly bejewelled women watching from a balcony, standing at a half-shut door or carrying a parrot's cage. The monumental, sculpted panel of the descent of Ganga at Mahabalipuram and the erotic

Intricately sculptured walls of the Khajuraho Temple.

Trimurti manifested in stone.

sculpture at Konarak and Khajuraho establish that the life-negating philosophy was not their credo.

Human and Animal Motifs

The earliest terracotta sculpture was small in size, but not without robustness and vitality. Moulding the human torso with massive strength and animals like bulls, showing rippling muscles and powerful limbs, was a tradition of concentrated strength that continued throughout the centuries, though later work sought out themes from the abundant legends of Hinduism.

- **Ten Incarnations** – Anticipating somewhat the great landmarks in the earth's evolution, the legend of the mighty boar rescuing the earth, which had been submerged, is probably a faint racial memory of the emergence of a vast landmass from under the armour of ice. The master sculpture of this incarnation in Udaigiri, Madhya Pradesh – with a massive torso striving upwards with an irresistible strength – has the delicately curved figure of the Goddess Earth resting on its shoulders. Other sculptures of the ten incarnations are found in Ellora,

Mahabalipuram and in the recently cleaned friezes of the Jagannath Temple.

Feminine Form

Alongside the capture of the masculine strength, Indian sculpture is successful in the evocation of the delicate, singing feminine line. The prime instance is the Didarganj Yakshi (second century BC): with homage paid to a full-breasted, sensuous woman, comparable to any creation of Titian or Rubens. In sculpting the dryad of Sanchi (first century), the girl is captured on the threshold of womanhood. Mathura (first century) produces a whole series of feminine figures: standing in delicate poses and sportive attitudes, in the happy company of birds, flowers, trees and gurgling streams.

Much later, Khajuraho (tenth century) once again emerges with the same lyricism of damsels: admiring own beauty in the mirror; writing love-notes; fondling a child; or lost in erotic embraces. The early and late Chola (ninth to thirteenth century) figurines of goddesses are as superb examples of supine beauty as the curvilinear figures of the gods like Shiva and Vishnu.

Low Relief

These sculptures display a marvellous capacity for storytelling with fluent ease, especially about the Bodhisattva or the Buddha on pillars, railings or walls, or, about Shiva, Vishnu or the mortal Krishna from the Hindu pantheon. A splendid sense of composition tackles and solves the odd-shaped spaces of sculpture, without any palpable sense of strain, within the contours available.

Spiritual Symbolism

Indian sculpture reached its greatest height in expressing spiritual qualities as evident in the figures of Buddha from the Gandhara era (first century) to the Gupta age (fourth–fifth century), marked by an idealised and subtle refinement of figure and expression.

Symbols played a profound role in the lion capital of Saranath (third century BC). It depicts four lions, back to back, facing the cardinal points as emblems of power and four racing animal figures – alternating with four wheels – that typify the whirling cosmos. They rest on a lotus: fountainhead of life and creative inspiration, with the whole seated on a crowning wheel motif, *Dharma Chakra,* as symbol of Universal Law. The same power of symbolism is seen a millennium later in the Chola period (ninth to thirteenth century) in the magnificent bronze image of Nataraja: the dancing Shiva: with an intense dynamism pulsating through the whole figure. Nevertheless, it is almost still in its balance, stable like the world with its gyrating galaxies and island universes.

Two points are worth noting about Indian sculptors. One, they have known how to creatively manipulate form and also to remain true to the inner vision. They, therefore, range all the way from realism to stylisation, which retain only faint suggestions of the natural forms. Second, they have been simultaneously sublime and grand in conception; and fine and charming in execution.

Deeply rooted in mythology and the belief in Hindu pantheon, the sculptors evolved their own techniques following *Shilpa Shastra* (art treatises) and excelled in both naturalistic and highly idealised idioms. The influence of Indian sculpture could be traced in Southeast Asia as well as in the Central Asian remains.

Handicrafts

The art of the craftsman, who transforms articles of daily utility into objects that are aesthetically satisfying, has been recognised in the Indian ethos for aeons. The early Indo-Aryans were attracted to beauty as an attribute to Godhead and in India – which is a cradle of a variety of handicrafts – beauty has been endowed with divinity and is worshipped. It was but natural that this reaching out to beauty and its manifold manifestations would be made a constant factor in the people's life. As a basic activity of Indian society, handicraft was as much an expression of the human spirit in material form, which gives delight to mankind, as any other visual art, described above.

The growth of handicraft has been the cultivation of sensitivity and the stirring of humanism. In order to bring elegance and grace into an otherwise harsh and drab human existence, the early Indian people ornamented first their person, then articles of everyday use, later their weapons, and finally their surroundings.

The rough and severe walls of their huts, the floors on which they sat, ate and slept, where they worshipped, all blossomed out in pictures. A strategic item like *dhanurban* (bow-and-arrow) became embellished with decorations as were *kumbha* (water pots). Alluring designs covered the mundane *randhana patra* (kitchen pans). Here the mere functional gets transformed into works of art, with the common becoming the cherished. Since no aspect of life was too insignificant to lay claim to beauty and sanctity, the special articles, used for particular occasions, in the way of clothes, ornaments, vessels, etc., acquired a certain standard: to ensure a high quality even in daily usage. The following attributes of handicraft are important:

- **Beauty –** This, as stated, remains the primary consideration: not merely in physical appearance, but also in concept;

Kashmiri craftmanship is renowned for exquisite and intricate patterns.

A sculptor at work.

Giving shape to earth.

- **Repetitive element –** This is prevalence of a set pattern. Where it is aesthetically excellent, the eye does not weary of the sameness;
- **Design –** This can be two- or three-dimensional, projected through form, texture and other variations in the object: by the interplay of light and shade. Combination of these factors makes for the rhythm and contributes to the psychological impact of an object;

- **Colour –** Since this can communicate vividly ideas and emotions, and has the power of vibration, craftsmen work out their own system: often unorthodox, differing from the prevailing concepts of colour and its role.

Among major genres of handicrafts are: pottery (called the 'lyric' of handicrafts because of its universal appeal); woodwork (with workmanship visible from household articles to the lumbering cart); stoneware (stone carving of icons) and eye-catching textiles.

An enormous variety in cotton, silk and wool was seen in earlier times, besides countless painted fabrics and embroidery; metal ware (covering religious images, ritual items and objects of utility); jewellery (distinctive and varied, artistic and elaborate, more than anywhere else); ivory (carvings and designs etched on the surface); basketry and mat weaving (essentially rural crafts, often with chequered-board patterns); *shola pith* (carvings made on *shola,* a white spongy material derived from a plant); toys and dolls (with fabulous folk and animal motifs); leather (with ingenious usage for decoration); glass (with quality of opalescence and glitter of diamond); folk painting (with a myriad varieties like *Madhubani, Worli, Pichwai, Patachitra,* etc.); and masks (especially for *Ram Lila* and *Chhau*), besides handcrafted musical equipments.

The span and quality of visual arts in India is indeed comprehensive and all pervading: ranging from the spiritual macrocosm to the household microcosm! There is beauty in form and simplicity in structure, resulting in harmony in design.

Folk paintings illustrating simple objects through bold designs and bright colours.

141

Chapter Eight
Performing Arts

Performing Arts

The Natya Shastra by Bharata, for the first time, revealed that rasa links art with aesthetic enjoyment. Rasa, it explained, was the response evoked by an artiste in the spectator's mind through his or her performance.

Manipuri dancer depicting a bhava *with elegance.*

The supreme beauty according to the Upanishads' way of thinking can be traced only in the ecstatic state realising harmony between the soul and Brahman: a perfect state of *rasa,* as an evoked state of delight and enjoyment. But the famous treatise on dramaturgy, *Natya Shastra,* by Bharata (second century) exposed, for the first time, an intimate link between art and aesthetic enjoyment called *rasa.* The arts mentioned in this treatise included music, dance and drama, apart from drawing, sketching and architecture. In being called the fifth Veda (literally the 'body of knowledge'), it was stated to have borrowed the chanting of mantras from the *Rig Veda;* singing from the *Sama Veda;* dancing and acting from the *Yajur Veda;* and *rasa* from the *Atharva Veda.*

Aesthetically speaking, *Natya Shastra* notes *rasa* as an emotional response of the spectator to what is emoted (*bhava*) by the performer on the stage: a psychological state, the content of which may be

Dance, as Bharata's Natya Shastra *explains involves an aesthetic expression of* bhava *through a combination of body movements and postures set to a rhythm or beat.*

pleasant or unpleasant, but the overall effect is of bliss and enjoyment.

There are eight *bhavas* (emoting of sentiment): *rati* (love); *hasa* (laughter); *shoka* (pathos); *krodha* (anger); *utsaha* (enthusiasm); *bhaya* (fear); *jugupsa* (disgust); and *vismaya* (wonder). The *rasas*, established or affected by *bhavas* in that order, are: *shringara* (erotic); *hasya* (comic); *karuna* (compassionate); *raudra* (angry); *vira* (valorous); *bhayanaka* (terrible); *vibhatsa* (nauseating); and *adbhuta* (wondering). The ninth *rasa* is *shanta* (tranquil), added later on. The stable emotions *(sthayi bhava)* are distinct from the thirty-three fleeting emotions *(sanchari bhavas),* such as hatred, boredom, doubt, alertness, aggressiveness, joy, sadness, vanity, impulsiveness, passivity, shock, and so on. Each *sthayi bhava* is, in fact, created out of these fleeting emotions (as ingredients and spices) and *rasa* is the ultimate relish from the taste of the *sthayi bhava!*

Dance

Natya Shastra gives a graphic account of *angika abhinaya* (physical movements) of the different parts of the dancer's body: head (thirteen), eyes (thirteen), neck (thirty-seven) and feet (ten). Even the minute details are analysed, for instance, in noting the slow movement of the head upward and downward, as distinct from its fast movement. The dancer's body movements and postures of a dancer include *chari* (movements), *bhramari* (turns) and *utplabana* (leaps), and then gloriously go into 108 *karanas* (primary body kinaesthesis) and 32 *angaharas* (combinatorial poses with *karanas*). The *vachika abhinaya* is the use of music, dialogue and exclamations to express thoughts, ideas and feelings, differentiating the language for separate classes of performers.

The *sattvika abhinaya* is the subtlety of the performer to express the innermost feelings through the facial gestures. The *aharya abhinaya* is the fourth constituent of dance: for ornaments, dresses, flower decorations and 'make-up'.

The visual effect of performing as well as communicating through music, dialogue and dance make it easy for the performer to express emotions and evoke *rasa* in the spectator. An actor or a dancer can perform by feigning an emotional situation and give a very semblance of a person in love or fear or anger, provided, she has got the performing skill. The natural way of speech or acting or performing is useful to depict day-to-day life, but the stylised speech or acting

Odissi dancer performing in a temple bearing lineage to the tradition of dancing before the deity.

Bharatanatyam, performed with Carnatic music, is one of the oldest classical dance forms of India.

temples that most classical dances of India nurtured and flourished. In the Hindu mythology, the celestials have their professional dancing girls *(apsaras)* and musicians *(kinnaras and gandharvas)*.

The *devadasis* (god's maids) and *vilasinis* were royally patronised in the Tanjavur and Andhra temples in the South: to dance before the deity. Called *maharis* in the Jagannath Temple in the North, similar god's maids danced in the sanctum sanctorum, with *gotipua* boys dancing outside the temple precincts. In the North, there were also *baijis* (pleasure women), adept in the performing arts who entertained the rich. In many ways, these were the torchbearers of the classical choreography tradition that carried the legacy forward for centuries.

Classical Dances

Classical dances of all regions go back for basic inspiration to Bharata's analysis for the aesthetics of dance. All classical dances have two main divisions. The first is *nritta,* which is intricate abstract dance, consisting of stylised movements and poses, working out complex rhythms without narrative or thematic content. The second is *nritya*: suggestive, expressive and interpretative dance, with every movement and gesture loaded with meaning. The interpretative style uses all the expressive resources of the body: facial expressions, hand and leg movements *(mudra and chari)*; and dramatic postures *(sthanakas)* of the body. Over the centuries, the gesture language has been refined to become one of the most expressive means of symbolic communication in eight classical dance styles. These styles, all of which have their set grammar and established sequence of performance items *(margam)*, are:

or performing has to be decorative and effective in its abstraction.

From the earliest times, dance was connected with worship and, alongside Vedic rituals and sacrifices *(yajnas)*, dancing played an important role. In later times, dancing before idols formed an essential part of daily worship in all well-known temples. Some of the great saints of India used to dance in ecstasy before idols. Thanks to the availability of the priests' patronage, it is in the

Kathakali dancer with elaborate costume and make-up.

- **Bharatanatyam** is known as *'Dasiattam'* in Tamil Nadu as practised by the *devadasi*s. It was consolidated as 'Bharatanatyam' only since the thirties of the twentieth century. Carried on the shoulders of individual gurus, dancers and institutions, Bharatanatyam is incredibly rich in the gesture language of body, face, hands and feet, using the side-wise knee-bend *(ardha mandali)* as its main stance.

  The 108 *karana*s depicted by the sculpted *nayika*s in the Chidambaram Temple precincts and similar ones by the Shiva statues inside the Brihadishwara Temple walls, provide strong inspiration to Bharatanatyam apart from the literary support for the same provided by Nandikeshwara's text *Abhinaya Darpana* (tenth century). Themes like *prem-shringar* and *bhakti-shringar* (eroticism and devotion), are created and groomed according to a historical order.

- **Kathakali** was derived as the popular form from the highly stylised dance-style *Kudiattam*, which uses Sanskrit language. It was confined to

Kuchipudi dancers perform in a quick and scintillating style in pace with Carnatic music.

highly mobile features of the dramatically enhanced face, which no mask can ever equal. *Nritya Lakshana Deepika* is a standard text used for this style as well as for Mohiniyattam.

- **Mohiniyattam** another Kerala-form, has softly undulating movements *(lasya)*, as opposed to Kathakali's vigorous virility *(tandava)*. While *lasya* and *tandava* are used in all classical dances, the movements here are like palms swaying and dancing in the breeze, resembling boats bobbing up and down in the backwaters of Kerala.

- **Kuchipudi** has been carried forward by the Brahmins of Andhra Pradesh, who are called *Bhagavatars*. It has survived essentially due to their earnest efforts to form itinerant groups, drawing inspiration from the folk form of *Yakshagana*. Resembling Bharatanatyam in many ways, it is a breezy and lascivious form, and adheres to its own repertoire of the stories from the *Bhagavata*.

- **Odissi** is another temple-based classical dance style, which has great antiquity to the Raja-Rani caves (second century) of Udaigiri complex in Orissa. Kept up entirely by *maharis* and *gotipuas*, it has been flourishing, thanks to the inspiration drawn from Orissa's exuberant sculptures on dance figurines and the sustained efforts and experiments made by many gurus and practitioners, having its own corpus of music.

the temple-stages *(Kutambalam)* of Kerala in the true *Natya Shastra* structure. It has a highly evolved body language of dramatic content, where even the *nava rasas* (nine emotions) can be most accurately portrayed by facial expressions. The costume and elaborate make-up (with the face painted over and the lips, eyebrows and eyelashes emphasised) differentiate good characters from the evil ones. Episodes from the two epics, Ramayana and Mahabharata provide themes for complete dance dramas.

The tumult or tranquility within finds immediate and heightened expression in the

Here the upper body is highly flexible and light, in comparison to the lower torso, with a rhomboid stance *(chauk)* defining the basic posture and the zigzagged body assuming curvilinear forms: twice-bent *(dwibhanga)*, thrice-

Folk dancers of Uttarakhand in colourful costumes.

bent *(tribhanga)* and multiple-bent *(atibhanga)*. The Oriya treatise *Abhinaya Chandrika* is the standard reference manual.

- **Kathak,** originally a temple-dance and accompanied by commentaries *(katha)*, is a vibrant form: in both its devotional and court-entertainment formats. Having its bastions in Lucknow, Jaipur, Varanasi, Vridavan (for *Ras Lila*) and partially Raipur, it dates its principal stance back to the erect and the single knee-bend of the Harappan figurine. While facial expressions are many and varied, hand gestures are few. The sheer multiplicity of abstract movements, sophisticated poses and intricate elaboration of rhythms, however, make Kathak a dazzling art form, with the accent perhaps on an intellectual delight. The technique is easily characterised by fast footwork, while the dance movement incorporates numerous pirouettes at great speed, invariably ending in statuesque poses.

- **Manipuri** developed around the worship of Krishna and performed in every Manipuri village in a temple dedicated to this god of love, song and dance have especially flowered in spiritually-rich group choreography known as *Ras Lila* in diverse forms. The technique of dancing is based on an interesting principle of 'compensatory rounded movement'. If the right hand is outstretched towards the right, the body tilts towards the left: in order to offset the right-side thrust. This is intriguingly different from the technique of Bharatanatyam in which, in the same example, the effort would be to emphasise movement to the right and obtain greater impact.

- **Sattriya** evolved in the early sixteenth-century Assam, under the neo-Vaishnavite movement of Shankara Deva. It was performed by monks in the *sattras* (place of devotional congregation). Having both *tandava* and *lasya* elements, the framework and contents, well preserved in the monasteries, follow the detailed hand gestures as described in Shubhankar's *Sri Hastamuktabali*.

Folk and Martial Dances

Rooted in the lives of the people, these dances, though have devotional origin, have become synonymous with the celebrations of the seasons as well as the flow of living: the season of plenty after harvest; the coming of rains or the spring, birth of a child; marriage of a daughter. The dance tempo varies over an astonishing range: from the slow, languorous swinging of the body in the dances of the Santhal tribals of Jharkhand and the people of the Himalayan Valleys to the boisterous jumps and leaps of the peasants of the Punjab and the wild, splendid whirls of the Rajasthan warriors to the exciting rhythms of the great drums.

There are also the endearing martial arts of the yesteryears: from *Kalari Payattu* of Kerala; *Thang-Ta* (sword-and-shield) of Manipur and *Rai Benshe* of Bengal to the codified varieties of *Chhau* which include Mayurbhanj's vigorous non-masked *Chhau*, Seraikela's gentle-masked *Chhau* and Purulia's virile masked *Chhau*.

Miscellaneous Forms

There are also some dance forms that are, while old, gradually getting codified and canonised, like *Gaudiya Nritya* of Bengal (following Shubhankar's *Sangeet Damodar*) and *Vilasininatyam* of Andhra (from the temple art of Andhra's *devadasi* community).

Music

Treatises from the second century onwards laid down elaborate modalities for the twin art of dance and music. The unstruck sound *(anahata nada)* was said to be heard as the vibration of space, when one let go of all inhibitions and preconceived notions, attaining a sense of liberation from the senses and becoming one with the god. Music was conceived as inseparable from meditation and contemplation, when the mind and muscles relaxed and gradually the whole body became an instrument resonating in consonance with the entire universe. Music thus is an alternative path of realisation: with the actual singing becoming a spiritual exploration, in addition to being an aesthetic one.

In keeping with the spiritual and religious heritage of the world, sound was used in multifarious ways to attain the ultimate metaphysical experience. From the earliest chants, the recited metrical hymns of the *Rig Veda* became the chanted, melodic songs of the *Sama Veda*. Known to have existed since Bharata's time, the *raga* was first discussed comprehensively in the eighth century in Matanga's *Brihaddeshi* and then in the thirteenth century in Saragadeva's *Sangit Ratnakar*. The notes, used for building up the melodic *raga,* were derived

Carnatic vocal music involves a melodious rhythmic expression of a devotional composition.

Dance being staged on the occasion of Holi in Bihar with performers enacting the spirit of the festival.

by their appeal to the aural aesthetics and not by a geometrically divided scale as in the West. Starting from three fundamental 'self-generated' *(swayambhu)* notes, the latter increased in number to five and then to seven: for building up melodies. The scale, as it finally evolved, was an octave: with a *madhya saptak* (middle one) supported at two ends by a *mandra saptak* (lower octave) and a *tar saptak* (upper octave). More minutely, each octave has 22 microtonal steps *(shrutis)* of less than a semitone.

Classical Tradition

The classical *raga* came into practice as freely improvised melody: using a fixed series of five, six or seven notes in the *aroha* (ascent) and *avaroha* (descent) through the octave and *pakad* (specific note-combinations). The *raga* is woven within this framework, where the singer remains his own composer and each singing concert becomes a supreme exercise in improvisation. In the initial stage, the singer contemplates the beatitude of the *raga's* timeless existence through the *alap* (elaboration), which alone can show music's pure and abstract elements. In the advanced stage, the singer comes to *bandish* (composition) proper, sensing the excitement of the rhythm of cosmic existence, as it were. While in the North *dhrupad* follows *alap*, in the South it is *keertan*. Solemnly devotional, *dhrupad* (derived from 'dhruva pad' or 'fixed stanzas') has a counterpart in *dhamar*, belonging to the Mathura region and related to Krishna's amorous exploits. *Khayal* (literally, a 'whim') has a design reminiscent of filigreed architecture, besides its relaxed tempo and laid-back manner of presentation.

As part of India's rich heritage of highly evolved music systems, Hindustani music belongs to the North, East and West, while Carnatic music prevails in the South. Both traditions use the *raga* as their foundation. Ammanacharya (fifteenth century) gave the Carnatic music its format of *kriti*, with distinct sections of *pallavi, anupallavi* and *charanam* still followed. Purandara Dasa (sixteenth century), hailed as *Sangita Pitamaha*, shaped the music from preliminary exercises up to concert-worthy compositions. Kshetragna (seventeenth century) garbed devotional *padams* with romantic or even erotic sentiments.

In the eighteenth century appeared the 'Trinity' of Tygaraja, Muthuswami Dixiter and Shyama Sastri, and their compositions in the form of ragam-tanam-pallavi with a distinguished lineage of *vaggeyakars* (poet composers) who are extant till today. Carnatic music—with its *raga alapana* (melodic exploration), *tanam* (melodic-rhythmic exercise), *neeraval* (creative melodic exploration) and *kalpana swara* (melodic-rhythmic exercise with notes)—has never looked back since, where devotion has always found a dominant role.

Light Classical Tradition

This covers *thumri* from eastern Uttar Pradesh and *tappa* from the Punjab, besides the seasonal varieties like *dadra, chaiti, jhoola, kajri, sawani, bara masa*. The social urge behind the coexistence of the above kinds of music is unmistakable: making a transition from the abstract and religious to the concrete and secular, with the prominence shifting from the melodies to the lyric. *Kritis* (set songs) in the South and *bhajan-keertan* (devotional songs) in the North are popular styles of religious music, usually with superb poetry depicting Rama or Radha-Krishna episodes.

Folk Tradition

Brihaddeshi recognised the large and inclusive category of people's music, also giving a list of classical *ragas* derived from the folk tradition. Even during the *Sama Veda* chants, there were folk songs like *grama geya* (songs in the hamlets) and *aranya geya* (songs in forests). These spontaneous melodies proliferated in course of time to envelop the entire life of man in an entrancing shell of musical sound: helping him to forget the tedium of work in the fields; touching with poetry the sacramental moments of marriage and its fruition in the advent of progeny; and lending wings for his flight in prayers to his creator. Like the seasonal songs, mentioned above, they kept man in touch with the creation and the Creator.

Drama

The earliest information on performance in ancient India is the *Natya Shastra* (second century), which treated the physical space of the theatre as basic to the structure of the play: its content, form and technique. Meticulous measurements were indicated for the ground plan of an edifice – complete with greenroom, backstage, front-stage, side-entries and auditorium – for establishing emotive and psychic correspondence to the micro-cosmos. A vertical pillar marked the centre of the stage as the most consecrated space and was worshipped during the play's beginning.

In place of Aristotelian unity of time and space, multiple scenes in different areas of the stage – all parts of the larger visual picture – were the norm, which resembled the simultaneous and sequential ritual acts in different areas of the sacrificial site *(yajnashala)*. Movement from one demarcated area to the other was analogous to the movement-curve and action plan of the sacrifice *(yajna)*, with dramatic action taking place in a cyclic rhythm, again like the *yajna*. These held for the highly developed Sanskrit dramaturgy, right into the second millennium.

In an unbroken canvas of the oriental tradition, *natya* (drama) implied a convention, namely, the artificial nature of life where ordinary reality was alluded to, through hints and nuances, symbols and metaphors. In the earliest recorded dramatic performance of the highly allegorical *samudra*

manthana, alluded to in Bharata's *Natya Shastra,* the action symbolises the conflict between the gods and the demons, with the triumph of the former at the end. Even here, the actor polarises light so as to make a literary background almost imperceptible!

According to Bharata:

> There is no maxim, no learning, no art or craft, no device, no action, which is not found in the drama. The latter is the confluence of all the departments of knowledge, different arts and various actions.

Such a dramatic tradition continued in India for about a thousand years in the first millennium, culminating in what is referred to as the classical Sanskrit theatre: with plays of Kalidasa, Bhasha and others. Then it gradually faded away, perhaps due to Islamic incursions from the North and West. Many of the modern dramatic works show an astonishing continuity with the earliest *natya*.

There was always a parallel tradition of bards, storytellers and nomadic singers who served a meaningful role in society and creatively transmitted the epics Ramayana and Mahabharata, and the Puranic tales: to commemorate festive occasions and agricultural-cycle rites, all of which are common throughout India today. These festive traditions are explained below.

Home Performance

Usually confined to the family and private in nature, these are connected with the *samskaras* (rites of passages). Many of these performances are accompanied by songs sung by household women. Most Hindu communities have songs earmarked for various stages of the life cycle, for instance, for the marriage–pregnancy–birth part there is the Marathi *palna* (cradle song) describing the first twelve days after birth; again, there are songs related to the birth of a child, particularly those describing the birth of Lord Krishna, as in a Rajasthani *halariyo* (lullaby).

Community Performance

Using such venues as central village-square, temple-precinct, garden or just the street, they attract densely packed crowds on occasions like religious festivals, weddings, harvests and important visits by outsiders. Instances of such dramatic pageants are *Ram Lila* in Uttar Pradesh (especially at Ramnagar), *Krishna Lila* in Orissa (with travelling performers from the Valmiki community) and *Ras Lila* in Uttar Pradesh and Manipur, usually based on the episodes from the Ramayana, the Mahabharata and the Puranas. Romantic ballads on young lovers like *Dhola-Maru,* are sung by the *langa* musicians of Rajasthan, while the semi-historical story of *Alha-Udal* is sung in the Uttar Pradesh and the epics or Puranic stories are narrated by the clapper-wielding *das kathiya*s of Orissa. Indeed, many community events involve mythological, historical or romantic narratives in some form or the other. In Bengal, the *patua* performers make use of serial *patas* (small paintings) and in Rajasthan, *padh* (very long scroll painting) is hung behind the *bhopa–bhopi* (male–female) performers, whose narration, singing, instruments (like *ravanahatta)* and dance are collectively used to tell tales of valour of the fourteenth-century Rajput chief, Pabuji. In Manipur, trance chanting by the *maiti*s at the *Lai Haraoba* festival uses extraordinary techniques of voice production: undoubtedly designed to communicate with not men, but God.

Public Performance

Certain community events are taken out of their original environments and presented to a wider, more heterogeneous base. The *Ram Lila* of Ramnagar is a classic example, where the performance action takes place at a number of different sites and the procession from one venue to the other is quite a part of the show. In reality, many regional performance traditions are public events, although they remain regionally rooted mainly due to the language used. Some dramatic forms in regional languages, which invariably incorporate songs, dance and instruments are: Maharashtra's *lavani* and *tamasha;* Rajasthan's *khayal;* Gujarat's *bhavai;* Kashmir's *bhand;* Uttar Pradesh's *nautanki* and *bahr-e-taved;* Bengal and Orissa's *jatra;* Assam's *ankiya nat;* Karnataka and Andhra Pradesh's *yasksha gana;* and Orissa's *prahlada natakam.*

In Orissa, the *lilas* like *Ram Lila, Krishna Lila, Radha Prem-Lila* and *Bharata Lila* as traditional theatre forms representing the deeds of the gods, saints and noble personages are distinct and different from each other. Similarly, various *naats,* namely, *Danda Naat, Bandi Naat, Desia Naat* and *Chadhia Naat* are derivations of *natya* and, like all ritualistic storytelling traditions prevalent in India, are continued till today.

In particular, *Desia Naat* uses a unique mask – with the entire head and face going in – which is presently only performed in Bali Island in Indonesia. The two-person *das kathiya* and six-person *pala*s are ritualistic plays: with everybody in full regalia.

Puppetry

Puppetry, in India, is used universally in a theatrical art form as a channel of human communication, cutting across physical barriers, political frontiers and linguistic constraints. Its antiquity is proven by ancient records as in the Tamil poet Thiruvallavur's famous work *Kural* (second century BC); Ilango Adigal's *Silappadikaram* (second century AD); Dhanapala's *Tilak Manjari* (eleventh century AD); Sri Vidyaranya's *Panchadasi* and Somnath's *Basavan Purana* (twelfth century AD); besides works by the poet Arul Nandi Shivacharier (thirteenth century AD). Ramayana and Mahabharata are replete with mention of puppets and puppet-like characters.

Regarded as celestial creations, all Indian puppets have been symbolic and stylised, without following the human anatomy. Traditionally regarded as the homeland of puppets, India abounds in puppeteers coming from all communities and religions, but usually from the lower strata of society. The faces and dresses are typically fashioned after the local customs. The traditional puppets derive their dramatic repertoire, costume and music from the folk theatre of the region: with distinctive mythological, historical or social themes.

- **Glove Puppets** are manipulated with gloves worn on hands. They are generally used in open-air performances. In Kerala, traditional *Pava Kathakali* or *Pava Kuthu* uses the storyline,

Puppets in Rajasthan displaying an exuberance of colours.

costume and music of Kathakali. In West Bengal, *Bener Putul* has puppeteers from the class of palanquin-bearers, performing to popular songs during a show. In Orissa, *Sakhi Kundhei* or *Gopalila Kundhei* shows the dalliance of Krishna with Radha. In Uttar Pradesh, the fast-disappearing tribe of puppeteers shows *Gulabo-Sitabo,* the quarrel between the wife and mistress of a man.

- **Rod Puppets** are manipulated from below, with puppeteers hidden behind a black curtain. In

West Bengal, *Danger Putul* takes theme, costume and music from *jatra,* the popular folk form of Bengal. In Orissa, *Kathi Kundheri,* manipulated from below with chords, also follow the *jatra* tradition of Orissa. The *Yampuri* puppets of Bihar run on wheel-boards inside a trench and showcase the aftermath of death.

- **Shadow Puppets** are presented in villages, in specially erected stages with white screens, shadow puppeteers perform from behind the

Kathputli show.

scenes and take themes from the regional versions of the Ramayana and Mahabharata, with shadows in colour. Performances are held commonly in fairs and festivals: to bring rains; to induce fertility to the soil for good crops; and to remove pestilence and cattle diseases. In Andhra Pradesh, *Tholu Bommalatta* uses dance steps in Kuchipudi style, while costumes are taken from the folk form *Yakshagana*. The Nellore leather puppets are the tallest in the world, being over seven-feet high. In Karnataka, *Togalu Gombeatta* has the northern puppets with beards and the southern ones with Hindu faces. In Kerala, *Thol Pava Kuthu* stage performances connect with temple rituals. In Tamil Nadu, *Tholu Bommalattam* is the same as its namesake in Andhra Pradesh, the only difference being that the former uses smaller puppets. *Chamdiyacha Bahuliya,* as known in Maharashtra, has many interesting buffoon characters which enact only from the Ramayana, like their counterparts in Kerala. Only in Orissa, *Ravana Chhaya* is in black-and-white, with puppeteers believing that Rama with his spiritual aura, casts no shadow, unlike the evil character Ravana.

- **String Puppets** are perhaps the most common form of Indian puppetry. They are manipulated by strings from above, akin to the Western marionettes. In Rajasthan, *Kathputli* puppets are the oldest form: manipulated by the Bhat community with characteristic whistle-sound and squeaking voice. In Karnataka, *Gombeatta* is based on the folk form of *Yaksha Gana*. In West Bengal, *Tarer* or *Suto Putul* draw its content from the epics and the *Bhagavata Purana*, with themes taken from popular *jatra*. In Assam, *Putala Nach, Putala Bhaona* or *Putala Bhaoriya* take their story, music, costume and presentation styles from two folk forms: *Bhaona* and *Bhaoriya*. In Orissa, *Gopalila Kundhei* depicts stories of Radha-Krishna. In Tripura, *Putul Nach* resemble the West Bengal ones, with cartoon-like tales based on the folk character 'Mona'. In Manipur, *Laithibi Jagoi* shows the stories of Krishna.

In Maharashtra, *Kalasutri Bahuliya* showcases the Ramayana: from the birth of Rama till the killing of Ravana. In Andhra Pradesh, *Koya Bommalatta* or *Sutram Bommalu* or *Keelu Bommalattam* is mostly seen in the temple festivals at Tripurinithura. In Tamil Nadu, *Bommalattam* uses stories from the epics. In Jharkhand and West Bengal, the santhal tribes practise *Chadar Badar*.

The variegated scene of performing arts in India is redolent with a many-splendoured beauty and some of the most subtly perceived aesthetics. However, their transcendental roots furrough the ground very well. Till recent times, every classical dance performance is a prayer by the danseuse, every classical and folk musician perceives the presence of a divinity, every theatre performance still works out its stylisation – even unconsciously – according to many of Bharata's tenets, and every traditional puppet is an emblem of the numinous power to the puppeteer: ever held in reverence.

In India, the still water of spirituality indeed runs deep.

Chapter Nine
Festivals

Festivals

Set in the lunar calendar and often associated with the worship of special deities, each festival is associated with exuberance, and gives a fresh lease to the cycle of life and death.

Bhakti Yoga lays down the path of indentifying oneself with God through faith and devotion.

In the year's twelve months, as the saying goes, there are thirteen festivals in the Hindu almanac! These festivals happen all the year round: to mark mythological events, celebrate changing seasons and even commemorate historical occasions and important anniversaries. Each festival gives a new meaning to the life cycle. The general tenor of these festivals is an extraordinary degree of bonhomie, where all reservations crumble and the spirit of camaraderie prevails. Apart from the general atmosphere of conviviality and exuberant joy, there are exchanges of gifts and sharing of sweets, as gestures of universal goodwill.

Worship

While celebratory occasions in the Vedic times were marked by *yajna* (sacrificial fire) as tribute to the cosmic forces as deities, the later Hindus, especially in the South, performed *puja* (worship) as ode to the Puranic gods and their icons. In a remarkable spirit of syncretism, both *yajna* and *puja* were seamlessly

Deepavali symbolises the victory of good over evil and the onset of good fortune.

amalgamated over time and are continued together to this day. Major festivals, dedicated to the emblems of divinities, are discussed below.

Deepavali

Occurring on the new moon night of October–November, it marks the return of Rama to his capital, Ayodhya, after fourteen years of exile. The night preceeding Deepavali celebrations is marked by lighting five lamps as is the practice in the North, or fourteen lamps as in Bengal. The evening of Deepavali is marked by an exuberance with the entire households (even the humblest of huts) lit up with earthen or brass lamps, and the bursting of firecrackers (reminiscent of the Guy Fawkes' Day in the UK).

Alongside the worship of Lakshmi, the Goddess of Wealth, there is *Deepotsava* (festive illumination) observed in temples, as well as all sacred places of worship and riverbanks to symbolise the spread of spiritual glow all around. Everybody adorn themselves with new clothes, especially the ladies wear the best of ornaments, capturing the social mood at its happiest. All the illumination and fireworks, joy and festivity signify the victory of divine forces over those of wickedness.

Deepavali is celebrated through many festivities in different parts of India and spreads across several days. In the South, on the previous day to Deepavali, worshippers take an early morning bath (*Ganga snanam*) and wear new clothes. The previous night in the North is spent away in gambling:

in anticipation of good fortune in the new year, beginning the next day. This is an echo of the ancient ritual of gambling on the new year's day for Dame Luck. In Bengal, the worship of Goddess Kali is held synonymous with Deepavali, as is the destruction of the Demon Narakasura in the South one day before. In the North, Dhanteras is celebrated two days before Deepavali to honour the divine physician Dhanwantari, as propitiation of good health in the coming winter and as thanksgiving for protection against the ailments during the monsoons that have gone by. Two days after Deepavali follows Bhratri Dwitiya, or Bhai-duj, a ceremony where the sister secures her brother's invincibility, recalling the myth of Yama and his sister Yami.

Holi

Touching the point of highest popularity, after Deepavali, it marks in March the end of severe north Indian winter. Holi witnesses uninhibited enthusiasm to spread coloured water and powder on

Lathmar Holi is celebrated at Barsana in Mathura, Uttar Pradesh, with extreme enthusiasm.

all and sundry, renewing friendly ties and burying old enmities. Perhaps reminiscent of ancient fertility rites, the two-day festival has a lesser day (Chhoti Holi) of receiving lotus seeds and dried fruits, especially by children. An evening bonfire is kindled by burning the Demoness Holika's effigy, with castaway things of the yesteryear set aflame. The second day marks the real celebration (Badi Holi, Dhulhauti or Vasant Purnima): by sprinkling colours, consuming intoxicants, and singing and dancing to throbbing drumbeats, almost reminiscent of *Rig Veda*'s Vasanta Utsav, complete with food and drinks.

Navaratri and Durga Puja

The September–October new moon has a composite festival all over India. Durga Puja in Bengal and Orissa is a major celebration over five days: with images of five gods and goddesses on a single platform and of Shiva manifest on the top. Their totemic mounts like lion, peacock, mouse, swan and owl accompany them, in addition to the celebration of the autumnal nature through *nava patrika* (nine leaves). On Maha Shashthi (sixth day from the new moon), the Mother-Goddess Durga, with her progeny, is heralded through *bodhana* (invocation) and *adhibasa* (consecration).

On the three successive, auspicious days – Maha Saptami, Maha Ashtami and Maha Navami – the intensive worship continues, with the *sandhi* (confluence) of Ashtami and Navami held as particularly auspicious. There are daily *pushpanjalis* (flower offering); *bhog* (food offering to the gods); and morning–evening *arati* (adoration with lamp), along with continuous reading of the *Chandi Purana*

Artisans begin making idols of Durga months before the festival.

167

Durga Puja celebrations are held with pomp and gaity.

and mass feeding of the devotees. On the tenth day from new moon falls Vijaya Dashami when the goddess is given a ceremonial adieu till the next year, with much fanfare and shedding of tears.

Beginning on the new moon, Navaratri is a festival of nine auspicious nights almost in entire North India, mostly accompanied by day-long fasting. In Gujarat, it is accompanied by night-long colourful dances of *Dandiya Ras* (beating with sticks) and *Garba* (with swaying and clapping) by women dressed in their finery. Tamil Nadu observes *Bomma Kolu* where specially tiered platforms are built to display icons, toys and artifacts. Friends and relatives are invited to witness the display, when the women are given betel leaves, kumkum, coconuts and occasionally little gifts as auspicious offerings. The ninth day of Navaratri in the South is dedicated to the worship of Saraswati, the Goddess of Learning. All objects of learning like books, stationary and musical instruments are placed on a pedestal and worshipped.

The tenth day everywhere is a celebration of Dussera (Vijaya Dashami) marked by the immersion of the icons of Durga and the fiery burning of massive effigies of demons Ravana, brother Kumbhakarna and son Meghanada to the accompaniment of fireworks, signifying the triumph of the good over the evil.

Krishna Janmashtami
Celebrated in late July–early August, Janmashtami is the birth anniversary of Krishna in the prison-house of the Demon Kamsa. On the midnight between the first *(Krishnashtami or Gokulashtami)* and the second *(Kalashtami)* days, the birth of

Lord Krishna, whose birth is celebrated on Janmashtami.

Krishna is celebrated with pomp and élan. Delicacies are prepared from milk and curds that Krishna loved. The ceremony of *dahi-handi* (breaking a pot full of milk and its derivatives), held aloft, is a very popular feature on the second day. The devotees fast all day and take food at midnight after the hour of divine birth.

Rama Navami
Falling in March–April, it is the celebration of Rama's birth and observed with day-long prayers. It is one of the five *maha vratas* (important fasts),

A devotee offering bel leaves and pouring milk on the Shiva linga during Shivaratri.

Hanumana, a symbol of strength, love and devotion.

since ancient times, along with those observed for Janmashtami, Ganesha Chaturthi, Shivaratri and Durga Puja.

Ganesha Chaturthi

This festival centres on the elephant-headed god, Ganesha, who has the power to remove all obstacles and bless any new ventures. It is observed in Karnataka, Tamil Nadu, and especially Maharashtra in August–September. Like Durga Puja in Bengal, it takes the shape of community worship in Maharashtra. Images are installed at various centres and worshipped with fervour for five, seven or eleven days. Ganesha's favourite sweet (*Modaka*), made of jaggery and coconut, is wrapped in rice flour and steamed and distributed amongst the devotees, before the image is immersed in the sea.

Shivaratri

It occurs in February–March when prayers to Shiva, fasting and penance for past sins are a must for devotees, marked by a night-long vigil and ritual worship to commemorate the night when Shiva first manifested himself in a towering phallic form with a flaming crown, said to be unfathomed by Vishnu and Brahma.

Vasanta Panchami

It is a spring festival held in February, in honour of Saraswati, the Goddess of Learning, in the North, though other gods are also propitiated. The colour yellow is dominantly used and, in Bengal, it is the time to initiate a child into education through several rituals.

Hanumana Jayanti

Celebrating the birth of Hanumana, as the most important devotee of Rama, it is observed in April. Hanumana is worshipped as the avatar of Shiva and as a true karma-yogi, a believer of selfless service. A special favourite of long-distance drivers and passengers in the North, the occasion is marked

Ratha Yatra in Puri, Orissa, is celebrated with great enthusiasm when devotees throng to get a glimpse of the deities and touch the auspicious rope pulling the chariots.

Women celebrating Teej, the Festival of Swings.

by decoration of vehicles with flowers and joss sticks, and recitations from the Ramayana and Hanumana Chalisa (forty verses in his praise).

Ratha Yatra

Especially observed in Orissa and other places of Krishna worship in June–July, the occasion witnesses the taking out of the icons of Jagannatha, along with his brother Balabhadra and sister Subhadra and worshipped as an unusual trinity in massive chariots, drawn by frenzied crowds in mammoth processions and attended amongst great festivities.

Vishwakarma Puja

A special feature of the Hindu value system is paying an obeisance to teachers and masters of art and craft. It comes in September–October when one's arms, tools and instruments of trade are honoured. On this occasion, dedicated to the divine architect Vishwakarma, a student worships his books, a blacksmith his hammer, a clerk his pen and a soldier his gun.

Varalakshmi Puja

Performed in honour of Lakshmi (Goddess of Prosperity) in most Shiva temples in Tamil Nadu, like in Thiruninrayur, Thiruvadi and Thiruvarur, it is held in late August. A silver face of Lakshmi tied to a coconut and placed on a *kalasha* decorated with a silk skirt and flowers is worshipped.

Bhadrakali Amman Puja

This eleven-day festival held in Pondicherry in May–June, honours the Bhadrakali Amman manifestation of the Mother-Goddess Parvati. The Bhadrakali Temple is a rare symbol of women's empowerment, as Parvati vanquished two fierce demons here, although blessed otherwise by her husband Shiva.

Rites

Major festivals that are based on ritualistic practice (often of folk origin) and with a strong root in the community are discussed below.

Lai Haraoba

Held in Manipur in April–May, it marks the amalgam of Shaivaism and pre-eighteenth-century tantric cult in religious ceremonies where music, dance and sports blend harmoniously.

It is a festival of the gods invoked in Meiti dialect by the Maibi priests and priestesses where their dance re-enacts the wedding of *Nongpok Ningthou* (Shiva) and *Panthoibi* (Parvati), consecrating newly-levelled earth to symbolise the creation of the cosmos by nine gods and seven goddesses.

Ras Lila

This is a mystic dance ceremony, mainly in Manipur and Vrindavan, held five times a year, re-enacting the dance of Krishna and the *gopi*s (milkmaids). It symbolises the universal manifestation of the god where each *gopi* is a favoured partner of Krishna and the message is that all human beings are equally beloved by the divinity.

Some variations of the Ras Lila are: *Vasanta Ras* (which is held during spring time); *Nitya Ras* (which is staged every day); *Kunja Ras* (which is held in gardens); and *Maha Ras* (which is staged with every *gopi* partnering Krishna).

Bhaiduj, like Raksha Bandhan symbolises sister-brother bonding.

Teej

It is held in June–July, when the women in Rajasthan, Delhi, Haryana and Uttar Pradesh herald the rains by suspending swings from trees and playing and singing for Mother Parvati celebrating her union with her husband.

Karwa Chautha

It is held in mid-October, when women fast and pray all day-long for the well-being of their husbands. They break their fasts only after sighting the moon in the evening.

Karadayan Nombu

Celebrated in mid-March, this is a solemn ceremony by women in Tamil Nadu, commemorating the legendary Savitri's triumph over Yama (God of Death) and re-claiming her husband from the dead.

Special *adai*s (bread and butter) are offered to god and eaten with homemade butter. Married women also tie yellow thread around their necks for the welfare of their husbands.

Raksha Bandhan

Celebrated in the North in September, it is held to reinforce the bonds between the brothers and sisters. In an act of symbolism, the sister ties *rakhi* (silk or cotton amulet) on her brother's wrist and prays for his prosperity and safety. In return, the brother gives her a token gift, recognising his protective role.

The festival derives its importance from the turbulent history of the North, when women often were victimised and needed protection.

Vaisakhi, the harvest festival of the Punjab is celebrated with fun and frolic.

Kartigai

It has the same significance as Raksha Bandhan, when sisters light lamps for the well-being of their brothers. It is observed in December in Tamil Nadu and other southern states, and a number of earthen lamps are lit and placed at the entrances to homes; as is done during Deepavali in the rest of the country. In the myths, Murugan (Lord Kartikeya) was born on this day and conceded the sister's right on brother's assets. *Maha Ras* is performed on this day with multiple Krishnas and Radhas.

Mattu Pongal

Also called Kanu Pongal, it is celebrated in the South by sisters for the welfare of their brothers. This is held on the second day from Pongal when the *Medu* (cattle) are worshipped.

Chaitra Purnima

Observed on the full moon in March–April in the South, it is a ritual ode to Chitragupta, the scribe to Yama (God of Death). His records are believed to keep a tally on people's good and bad deeds, deciding on an individual's reward or punishment. In particular, the bronze statue of Chitragupta is taken out in procession at the ancient Chitragupta Temple at Kanchipuram near Chennai.

Nature

Some festivals are related to the rhythm of nature and life cycle. These are often of regional origin:

Vaishakhi

It is a traditional thanksgiving festival when the *rabi* (summer) crop is harvested in April–May and

Onapookkalam *(carpet of flowers)* is made during Onam out of flower petals and foliage.

generally earmarked for an auspicious beginning of the regional New Year. The Punjab has carnivals with boating, swimming and wrestling bouts on riverbanks, accompanied by resplendent dances: vigorous *Bhangra* for men and soft *Gidda* for women. Tamil Nadu and Kerala have Vaishakhi as New Year's Day celebrations as has Bengal terming it *Naba Barsha* (New Year): associated also with Buddhism and Sikhism.

Yugadi

The New Year's beginning in the mid-March for Andhra Pradesh is *Yugadi*. A seasonal, nutritious chutney is specially made out of new neem flowers, fresh green mangoes, *gur* (jaggery) from fresh sugarcane and new *chintakaya* (tamarind), to savour the season's first flavour!

Gudi Padva

This is Maharashtra's New Year's Day, on the same day as *Yugadi*. Traditionally, a long pole – tied with

a *khand* (blouse piece) to hold an earthen pot on the top – is erected outside the home for worship, and new clothes and tasty food add to the spirit of fun and frolic.

Vishu and Pooram

Vishu is Kerala's New Year's Day when greetings and gifts are exchanged. An auspicious omen, *kani*, is made out of coconut and paddy, and tied with golden cloth and ornaments. Yellow laburnum is made in the morning. Pooram is celebrated after Vishu, in honour of Shiva, in temples of Kerala: with processions of gaily-caparisoned elephants. The Vedakkunatha Swamy Temple in Trichur and Shiva Temple in Vaikkom are known for Pooram, whose highlight is the rushing forward of the elephant bearing the *utsava murthy* (processional statue) of Kartikeya so that it can pay obeisance to the Vaikkom elephant.

Onam

Celebrated in Kerala during August–September as a festival of rain and harvest among all communities and all religious groups, it witnesses the streets being decorated with flowers. This is to welcome the ancient king Mahabali amongst feasting (with special delicacies like *pongal* and *aviyal*) and much merrymaking. The *Aranmula Uthratadi Vallamkali* (snake-boat racing) is an annual event during Onam at Aranmula, Kottayam and Champakulam.

Puli Kali (or *Kaduva Kali*) is a part of Onam celebrations when performers paint their bodies with bright yellow stripes and take the guise of

Ardha Kumbha Mela at Allahabad.

Bihu dance: women join in joyous celebration of spring.

tigers. Other festival dance performances include: *Kummatti Kali* (mask dance); *Thumbi Thullal* and *Kaikotti Kali,* besides the ubiquitous Kathakali.

Makara Sankranti

An important festival in mid-January, it is preceded on the previous night by Lohri (bonfire), into which is thrown harvest produce like sugarcane stalks, parched rice and sesame seeds. On the Sankranti day in the North, *khichdi* (mishmash of rice, lentils and vegetables) is prepared and given in charity. Sankranti, signifying light, gives the message of intellectual illumination. It is the *viveka* (discriminatory wisdom) – to choose between the right and the wrong – that is believed to lead man on to the path of happiness.

Pongal Sankranti

Observed in the South, between 13–15 January. It is celebrated mainly in Tamil Nadu, Andhra and Karnataka. As a harbinger of *uttarayana* (the sun's northern course), it symbolises profuse light and warmth, and is marked by distribution of sesame seed and jaggery. While sesame seed stands for companionship, jaggery denotes sweetness of speech and demeanour.

Kumbha Mela

Every twelfth year on the Makara Sankranti day, this mega *mela* (fair) takes place as one of the most inspiring testimony of the intrinsic cultural unity of the Hindu world.

Held, by rotation, in Allahabad, Haridwar and Ujjain, nearly ten million people – of all castes and creeds, sects and languages, saints and commoners – converge for a holy dip in the river. There is also an Ardha (six-yearly) Kumbha Mela, held at half that interval, with similar rituals but far less pomp.

Gangaur

Celebrated in Rajasthan during March–April, it is a month replete with festivities. Ostensibly to honour the Mother-Goddess Gauri (Parvati), the golden-complexioned consort of Shiva, the women observe fast, keep a night-long vigil and share stories about Parvati.

Dressing in their best and walking in musical processions, they hold clay images of Gauri on their heads which then are immersed in a river or lake. In Udaipur, there is a Gangaur fair where young boys and girls are allowed to meet and choose their life-partners: without parental interference. In Jodhpur, Gangaur (also called *lotiya*) women carry *lota*s (brass water pots) for miles to fetch water in.

Bihu

The most important festival in Assam, it reflects nature, youth and fertility cult and is observed throughout the state: irrespective of caste, creed, language and religion. There are three variations: *Bhogali Bihu* during winter in January–February when the harvest is gathered; *Kangali Bihu* during autumn in October–November when paddy is transplanted; and *Rangoli Bihu* during spring in March–April when the land is prepared for sowing. The spring ceremony brings out the colourful mood of nature worship and is accompanied with mass participation through music and dance. *Muga* (golden) silk, which is a prized product of Assam, is worn by everybody.

Personage

In a remarkable eclecticism, there is sustained regard in the Hindu polity for the luminous personalities who often parted ways from its tenets and gave rise to other faiths. The following major festivals include some of them.

Statue of Mahavira, the twenty-fourth Tirthankara, at Dilwara Jain Temple, Mount Abu, Rajasthan.

Guru Purnima

It is an ancient festival in June-July to honour the great Guru Vyasa – credited with wielding his pen for classifying the accumulated spiritual knowledge of the Vedas under four heads – *Rig, Yajur, Sama* and *Atharva*. To him also goes the credit of composing the authentic treatise of Brahma Sutras: to explain the background of the Vedas. He is also credited with the composition of the greatest of epics, the Mahabharata, embodying the immortal song of Bhagavad Gita and perhaps the eighteen Puranas, containing the stories of our great heroes and saints, and carrying their moral and spiritual precepts: to be observed with fast and prayers for wisdom.

Buddha Jayanti

Buddha Purnima (full moon) in end-May signifies three major events of the Buddha's life: birth in Lumbini (now in Nepal); salvation in Bodh Gaya; and death in Kushi Nagar. There is a solemn celebration of the event throughout the country, irrespective of caste and creed, when the Buddha's seminal contributions are remembered with reverence and prayers.

Mahavira Jayanti

Observed in end-April, this is in remembrance of the twenty-fourth Jain Tirthankara (prophet). The first Tirthankara Adinath initiated the faith and the twenty-third Tirthankara Parshanath preceded Mahavira. Also known as Vardhamana, he is regarded as the last one of twenty-four Tirthankaras and is one of the greatest prophets of peace, social reformation and non-violence.

Gauda Purnima

It is observed in February as the birth anniversary of the sixteenth-century Vaishnava saint-poet Chaitanya Mahaprabhu from Bengal, who brought the Vaishnavite renaissance in India, with epicentres in Nabadwip, Vrindavan and Puri. It is synonymous with the Holi. It is also known as Dol Purnima.

Guru Govind Singh Jayanti

Guru Govind Singh was the tenth and final Guru in the holy tradition initiated by the great saint Guru Nanak, who richly inherited the legacy of the fearless martyrdom of his father, Guru Tegh Bahadur and set the tenets of the Sikh faith on firm lines. Held in January, on this day, the community renders charity to the needy.

Thyagaraja Jayanti

The birth anniversary of the great composer-saint Thyagaraja of the South is observed in January–February. Thousands of his compositions, known as *kritis*, are sung in the annual assemblage of musicians at his birthplace Thiruvaiyaru in Tamil Nadu: to celebrate the anniversary.

This brief account of Hindu festivals does not cover other festivities like Narasimha Jayanti (April–May); Ganga Puja (June); Narmada Mata Puja (February); Lakshmi Puja (October–November); Govardhan Puja (October–November); Go Puja and Annakut (October–November); Jagaddhatri Puja (October–November); Kartikeya Puja (October–November); Valmiki Jayanti (October) and Guru Nanak Jayanti (November); among a few others. It also does not touch upon the omnipresent phenomenon of *vrata* (which involves periodic fasting and praying), observed singly or collectively by women, in the confines of their homes or community: to propitiate some minor gods and goddesses, such as Shani (to evade disaster); Satyanarayana (for family welfare); Shashthi (for bestowing children); Manasa (to protect against snakebite); and Santoshi Ma (for well-being).

Still, what emerges, as the major hallmark of festivals, is the unmistakable nature of public worship of deities or en masse observance of rituals or celebration of nature with infectious joy. Mass participation in an indefatigable spirit brings in a new elation and there is considerable elimination of the ego. These occasions are marked most often by a large-scale transcending of caste and creed-barriers, and partaking of the offerings *(prasadam)* in a community spirit: serving as a social and community bond. The major fulfilment is that of renewal of relations with the gods and nature, and re-assertion of a vitality that has stood the test of time.

Chapter Ten
Diaspora

Diaspora

Through trade, visits of scholars and migration of Indians over the centuries, Hinduism has evolved. Engaged with most of Southeast Asia and China, it has been enriched and has, in turn, enlightened these cultures through such exchanges.

Indonesian sculpture, showing marked Hindu influence.

Since ancient times, there has been voluntary and encouraged diaspora of energetic Hindus (followed by Buddhists and later Muslims, Parsees and Christians) from the Indian mainland to Southeast Asia and East Africa. Some authorities trace them even up to Mexico and Latin America: going by some remarkable similarities with the Maya and Inca civilisations. Here is a coherent re-construct of the Hindu diaspora.

Early Waves

India had contacts with the Far East (traced up to Philippine islands, as evidenced by the presence of distinct Vedic elements in Polynesia) as early as 2700 BC. This was during the Harappan period and the contact was maintained till the Vedic period ending 1500 BC. Some migrations took place around 1000 BC of the Mahabharata period, which were renewed in the fourth century BC under the Mauryas, particularly during the reign of Ashoka in the third century BC.

Ashoka dispatched monks to Suvarna Bhumi (greater Indian islands) mainly for proselytisation of Buddhism. Emigration movement took a bigger shape around the commencement of the Christian era and became an avalanche whenever India enjoyed comparative security and prosperity.

Myanmar

In the Arakan region, the Indian warriors had overpowered the local rulers and set up their own kingdom just after the Mahabharata period, with one of the two leaders of Indian warriors being a sanyasi. A prince from Hastinapura came to Brahma Desha (Upper Burma) to lay the foundation of his kingdom at Sri Kshetra (akin to Kurukshetra). According to another tradition, the forefathers of the Buddha came from the Shakya clan of Kapilavastu and settled in the upper valley of the Airavati (Irawadi) River. The Chinese province of Yunan, when ruled by the Hindu kings in ancient times, was called Gandhara Rashtra.

After the Shakya dynasty was destroyed, there came the warriors from the Ganga Valley who established their own kingdom. Their first ruler was a prince of Varanasi. In the Lower Burma, Indians from the Godavari and Krishna rivers crossed the sea in the remote past and settled in the delta land, along with its coastal region.

Java

Heroes of the Mahabharata, under the leader Aji Shaka of Hastinapur, claimed descent from Arjuna's son Parikshita, and colonised Yavadwipa (Java). Jyeshtha, a Brahmin, introduced Hindu worship, Indian language and Hindu law. Twenty thousand migrants from Kalinga sailed across the sea from the east coast of India and colonised the island. While some of them died due to pestilence and some returned, the rest remained in Yavadwipa. In AD 78, it was colonised by a prince of Gujarat, who came in a ship and established his kingdom in Yavadwipa.

Sumatra

As per tradition, Ashwathama, son of Drona, came after the Mahabharata period and established law and order among the warring tribes in Suvarna Dwipa (Sumatra).

Cambodia

Kampuchea (Cambodia), too, has its tradition connected to northern India. Prince Pradyumna of Indraprastha was banished by his royal parents and came to Kokatha Loka, after crossing rivers, trampling valleys and traversing mountains. Called 'Sundara Kumara' for his handsome visage, he married the beauteous Kinnari, daughter of the local tribal king and was enthroned. He expanded the kingdom and fought against Gandharva Loka to retrieve his abducted consort. The locals still point to the route that Indians used and recollect the evolution of their civilisation and culture. The legend of Sundara Kumara is still enacted in drama and enjoyed by the masses and the elite alike.

Sri Lanka

As per the *Mahavamsha Jataka* (second century BC), the King of Bengal had banished Prince Vijaya Simha, who came to Sri Lanka in a large ship with 500 warriors in the sixth century BC. They enforced

Continuity of rituals, reflecting the extent of influence in the diaspora.

claim descent from Rama, son of Dasharatha, who killed Dashanana (Ravana) for having kidnapped his goddess-like wife Sita. Indeed, the Annamese have their own Ramayana, as also each constituent of Indochina.

The diaspora of Indians in ancient times to the countries of Southeast Asia and the annals of those kingdoms by Hindu colonists were unlike the later European ways of colonisation. Among the European powers were the English, Dutch, French, Portuguese and Spaniards, who acted with explicit support of home governments and were accompanied by military forces to back them up to forcibly impose supremacy over the people of other countries: mainly to exploit the resources of the colony to the benefit of their homeland. In contrast, the Hindu colonists used the colonial resources for the benefit of the indigenous people. In fact, the Hindus actually enriched the colonial population by introducing the art of writing, imbibing high degree of civilisation and culture, language and literature, improved methods of cultivation, advanced engineering, art and science, improved handicraft and introduced new industries. By bringing education and learning under the guidance of organised administration on Indian lines, the Hindu colonists united the people under one cultural umbrella which was inculcated with national pride.

Indians went out of their country without any army and any sort of backing of any Indian state. Hindus left their motherland to settle abroad in colonies and not to make fortune and run back to their motherland. It was diaspora in the truest sense, where the penetration of Hindu civilisation,

law and order and Prince Vijaya was anointed as king with universal consent. The country was called 'Simhala' after him. The Indians settled for good after free intermarriage.

Vietnam
Called Annam by the Hindus, the main part of Vietnam, Tonkin, was under Hindu and Buddhist influence prior to second century BC. Although it remained a dependency of China for 1,000 years, the Annamese owe all their learning to India and

culture, language, law, customs, court manners and introduction of Indian languages in all Hindu colonies of Southeast Asia, including Kampuchea, took place so peacefully that the indigenous population never felt that their country had been taken over.

It remains a historical fact that scholars, priests, teachers, officials and princes went to Southeast Asia, Sri Lanka, etc., to be religious mediators, and to establish law and government. To boost trade and industry, guilds and corporations were organised – strictly on the lines of Hindu India – of various professional groups of ironsmiths, goldsmiths, carpenters, weavers, spinners, potters, mat-makers, farmers and dairymen, to whom government provided assistance to develop production and improve productivity and quality. *Gunadosha parikshaka* (quality inspectors) were appointed to enforce rules of standards as per the inscriptions with standardisation of goods, which originated in India, and were carried through during the Mauryan, Gupta and Chola times. Research was encouraged and Ayurveda developed. *Rugnalayas* (hospitals) were built and provided with *vaidyas* (doctors), medicines, nurses, beds, cushions and mosquito-nets, along with free food for all patients, whether Hindu, Buddhist or otherwise.

The Hindu diaspora in the cultural colonies in Southeast Asia was pragmatic enough to give full education to women and afford equal opportunity in their eligibility for administrative positions. In Kambuja (Cambodia), women magistrates were not uncommon. There were Brahmins and Kshatriyas, and intermarriage between the two was a very common affair. Their progeny, called *Brahma-Kshatra,*

was treated at par with Brahmins and Kshatriyas, including wedlock. According to inscriptions in Kampuchea, Shudras (including *Chandala*s) were conspicuous by their absence. Rulers were expected to study law in general and *Danda Niti* (Hindu penal law) in particular. The inscriptional evidence – on the environment of education, structure of administration, shape of social organisation, set of Hindu customs, promulgation of Hindu law and introduction of Hindu festivals – is an unmistakable pointer to the Hindu influences in the entire life and society of these countries, and bears eloquent testimony to a glorious period of unabated cultural exchange between India and these countries.

Incidentally, when Hindus migrated in ancient times, it took one complete year to cover the one-way sea-route from Tamralipta of Bengal or the Andhra east coast to Kambuja. In the absence of geographical knowledge of the interior and of the people living in Southeast Asia, establishing an intimate contact in such a vast region – from the Bay of Bengal to the Pacific Ocean – was in itself an uphill task and of unimaginably daring nature. To establish business on a firm footing in vastly wide-ranging, roadless spaces and capturing power in such foreign lands – at least 1,500 miles away from India – during the days of sailing ships and bullock-carts surely boggle the mind!

Middle Waves

The exceedingly cosmopolitan cultures of the Indic world were continued and sustained by the Buddhist and later Hindu kings as flag-bearers of Indian culture to the Southeast Asia in the second half of the first Christian millennium. Though Bali Island is generally

Golden Ganesha showing a marked resemblence to oriental art form.

'by the prowess of the emperor's own arms' and who needs to make submission 'for charter-bearing imperial seal'.

Srivijaya Empire (eighth–eleventh century AD)

Sanjaya, a Hindu king, founded a powerful state in Java in the eighth century, to be replaced later in the century by the Buddhist dynasty of the Sailendras, who installed themselves as the Maharaja of Srivijaya and controlled a vast empire. In the ninth century, the Hindu kingdom revived itself renewing its links with India.

The kingdom of Mataram was defeated in the early eleventh century by Srivijaya, but it revived again later in the century. By the fourteenth century, the Hindu kingdom of Majaphit in eastern Java had achieved considerable importance.

King Narasimhana III (ninth century AD)

Belonging to the Pallava dynasty, Narasimhana III had a powerful fleet of ocean-going ships. The evidence of his naval conquest is known from an inscription found in Thailand, which commemorated a sacred tank and temple dedicated to Vishnu and were managed by an established guild of Indian merchants, soldiers and cultivators: for religious usage and water storage.

Emperor Rajaraja Chola (eleventh century AD)

On the request of some kings, he fitted a naval armada to mount an attack on the Shailendras of Suvarna Dwipa (Sumatra) and occupied their capital city, but – following the generous Indian tradition – restored the kingdom to the defeated King Vijayottunga Varmana.

characterised as the Hindu 'paradise' in the Muslim Indonesia, the Prambanan Plains and their exquisite temples in central Java are a striking testimony of the influx of Hindu culture into all of Southeast Asia. Four such historical instances are discussed below.

Emperor Samudragupta (sixth century AD)

In his Allahabad pillar inscription, giving details of vassal kingdoms, mention is found of *Samudra-Paranta-Dwipantara* (group of islands, across the sea, separated from each other by sea), which is held

Borobudur Temple complex in central Java, a place for Buddhist pilgrimage.

During the course of the seventeen expeditions of Sultan Mahmud Ghaznavi (eleventh century AD) to India, a large number of people, many amongst them learned and scholars of repute, fled to the Hindu colonies in the East. Bakhtiar Khilji (eleventh century AD) completed the conquest of North India, after destroying the world-famous Nalanda University, and making a very large number of Hindus (and Buddhists) flee to Myanmar and beyond, mostly to Kambuja. The latter was ruled by the powerful Shailendra king Suraya Varmana I, a Buddhist, who showed equal reverence to Shaivism and Vaishnavism, and welcomed the Hindus with open arms.

Indeed, the demise of 3,000 teachers and 10,000 students of the Nalanda University – many among them were from Myanmar, Thailand, Kambuja, Champa, Yavadwipa, Suvarnadwipa, Simhala, Tibet, Nepal and Gandhara as well as Malayadwipa in the hands of the Khilji soldiers – caused en masse fleeing to any place out of India. The inferential evidence of the countries of Suvarna Bhumi proves such a diaspora. During the days of Khilji onslaughts, Kambuja under King Jaya Varmana VIII (thirteenth century AD) also admitted and supported a large influx from India.

As an outcome of this diaspora, the footprints of India's cultural links are visible quite distinctly till today: in diverse forms and manifestations. An enduring cultural landmark is the Ramayana, as one of the most popular epic stories: revered from Myanmar to Indonesia. Interestingly, the Ramayana is pronounced as 'Ramakien' in Cambodia and 'Lamakyan' in Laos, and presented by professional dancers. Notwithstanding variations and local specificities in the ways its characters are depicted, the basic theme of the epic is the same: presenting it as a powerful dance drama, invoking folklores and depicting an ideal image of rulers and their relationship with the people.

There are epic narratives from the Ramayana and the Mahabharata engraved on the walls of many major temples of the region, the most important of which are the Angkor Wat of Cambodia and Borobudur of Indonesia. In Laos, the old northern capital Luang Prabang has a number of Buddhist temples with paintings and engraved images of the Ramayana and the Mahabharata, while the southern cultural heritage site Champasak has

the ruins of Wat Phu Temple: where the Buddhist *vihara* coexists with icons of Vishnu and Krishna. These temples present an innovative synthesis of architectural designs of the Indian, Chinese and other Southeast Asian forms, with Angkor Wat and Borobudur clearly reflecting the patterns and ambiances of South Indian temples such as those in Mahabalipuram and elsewhere.

In Thailand, Laos and Cambodia, and partially in Indonesia, the national languages draw heavily from Sanskrit and Pali, and the individuals' names are largely derived from Hindu and Buddhist mythological characters. Many of their festivities bear a close resemblance to the Indian festivals. There are instances of boat races; worship of the River Mekong (akin to 'Ma Ganga') by floating oil lamps; and water festival – as a clone of the North Indian Holi – using water instead of colour.

Recent Waves

India also developed extensive links with central Asia, Aden and the Gulf, and the east coast of Africa over a long time, making for a happy inter-cultural co-mingling among Gujaratis, Hakkas, Cantonese, Malayalis, Arabs, Bataks, Achenese, Malayas, Minangs and Parsis. Indicated below is a short chronicle of contemporary diaspora that has continued unabated, under many favourable or often adverse circumstances.

Indian Ocean

Before the European hegemony commenced in the modern period, the Indian Ocean trading world provided conditions for a multi-cultural environment, and there is evidence of Indian settlements in East

Africa, extending back to the twelfth century. The Gujaratis established a diasporic presence early in the second millennium and were renowned for their entrepreneurial spirit, commercial networks and business acumen. They traversed the Indian Ocean with confidence. A Gujarati pilot had guided Vasco da Gama's ship to India.

After a temporary setback to the Indian Ocean trading system under the Portuguese rule, the Gujarati diaspora found a new lease of life under the British dispensation in the ninteenth century, migrating in large numbers to places like Kenya, Tanganyika, South Africa and Fiji. Mahatma Gandhi had observed how the early political

Lord Padmasambhava's statue in Namchi, Sikkim.

proceedings in South Africa were largely conducted in Gujarati language. In East Africa, where Indians helped to build the railway lines, their presence was so prominent that banknotes in Kenya, before the country acquired independence, had inscriptions in Gujarati. In present times, the Gujaratis also occupy positions as teachers and educators in many Muslim countries around the world.

The Caribbean

The singular misfortune of the greater number of Indians – who would become agents for India's magnificent diasporic presence – was to experience the world as indentured labourers: a disguised form of slavery. When slavery was abolished in the 1830s in the British Caribbean and labour shortages threatened to reduce plantation owners to bankruptcy, it became expedient to import labour: largely from the Gangetic Plains and present-day Tamil Nadu. While the first shipload of Indians arrived in Trinidad and Tobago (1845), others went to Guyana (1838) and Surinam (1873), and yet others to plantations in Mauritius. Indians came to Jamaica (1873), Mauritius (1834) and Grenada (by dispersal): mostly from Uttar Pradesh and Bihar – speaking primarily the Bhojpuri dialect – as workers. Initially, they were disillusioned not to have found promised working conditions. Nationalist opinion brought the indenture system to a close in 1917, though not before 1.5 million Indians had sold themselves into debt-bondage. They lived in appalling conditions: in the lines previously inhabited by slaves. These Indians humanised the landscape, tilled the soil and were the great, unsung heroes and heroines of the diaspora. The 'East Indians' today form a major ethnic group in the Caribbean and have shown their pioneering spirit in almost every field, while preserving their traditional value system.

Southeast Asia

As discussed earlier, Indian links with Myanmar, Indonesia and Thailand, and later to the Philippines, Hong Kong, Singapore and the states of Indochina have always been substantial, mostly from South India. The plantation Tamil workers went to Fiji and Malaysia: for rubber and sugarcane cultivation.

At the present juncture of history, the Indian diaspora gives rise to uncertainties as much as promises and accomplishments. A significant part of Indian Malaysians still live in and around plantations, with problems of alcoholism and marginalisation from the mainstream community. The Indo-Fijians accounted for over half of Fiji's population some years ago, but left the country in droves after the coups in 1987 and again in 2000. But the same diaspora has nurtured soft forms of Hinduism: in the genre of 'Chutney' music and the first ever novel written in Bhojpuri.

The USA and Canada

The USA has among the largest Indian diasporic population today, nearing 3.2 million. In the early twentieth century, students, Ghadarites and Punjabi farmers were exempted from the prohibition orders on the entry of Asians in the 1920s. Many Punjabi men married Mexican women.

The vast bulk of professional Indians arrived in the USA, following the immigration reforms of 1965. Though they occupy today a significant and visible place in the lucrative professions, Indians also ply taxis in New York and dominate the 'Dunkin Donuts' franchises across the country. The Patels' grip on motels is a truism, just as the corner shop in the UK, once a quintessential expression of 'Englishness', is now a Gujarati institution. The Indo-American lobby on Capitol Hill is becoming increasingly important.

Canada had a substantial influx of the Indians – particularly from the Punjabi farming community – since the 1930s. These sturdy men, mostly settled in Quebec and the inhospitable Vancouver region, have now flourished and acquired political voice in running the land.

About the performance of the diaspora in the USA, it will be a revelation to note that 38 per cent of the country's doctors are Indians; 12 per cent of scientists are Indians; 36 per cent of NASA employees are Indians; 28 per cent of IBM employees are Indians; 17 per cent of those from INTEL employees are Indians; 13 per cent from XEROX are Indians; and 23 per cent of the entire Indian community possess Green Cards!

Europe

The contemporary diaspora (1830) of Indians, comprising predominantly Hindus, is a more structured phenomenon in the UK. From the point of view of the permanent settlement of a distinctive Indian population overseas, the massive movement of Indians to Britain and, to some extent, French and Dutch colonies, and their flourishing social and business life – invariably contributing to the well-being of the settled countries – have followed the colonial rule in India until 1947. Even now, doctors

and nurses of Indian origin are predominantly present in the UK.

The common goal in the above diaspora of the Indians (mainly Hindus) was to gain prosperity, occupy an important role in the society and government, and maintain status and enduring Indian values. This is no mean achievement, in spite of the initial handicaps and owes a lot to the innate vitality of the Indian civilisation. The continuity of linkages in distant lands has been nothing but impressive and Indian migrants in countries of the West Indies, Fiji and Mauritius have carved out a niche in society for themselves, in consonance with the religious-cultural artifacts of India that they had carried with them.

The Indian diaspora, on the whole, showcases how resilient the parent culture actually is and how firmly it has been able to withstand the pressures of local customs and religious influences.

Chapter Eleven

Epilogue: Renaissance

Epilogue: Renaissance

Mark Twain mused: India is the cradle of the human race, the birthplace of human speech, the grandmother of legends and the great grandmother of tradition.

Shankaracharya, the fountainhead of Vedantic philosophy.

The most distinguishing characteristics of a renaissance are: its tolerant spirit of revival for the best values; enlightened interest in sciences and arts; a balanced approach to life and society; a resurgence to the future with a new vitality of mind; and an openness of approach. Looking closely at Hinduism as it has evolved in the past and is shaping its present, it will not be found lacking in most of these lofty attributes. Considering that India invented the numerical system in the first century BC and that Aryabhatta invented the zero, here is a generous tribute paid by Albert Einstein:

> We owe a lot to the Indians, who taught us how to count, without which no worthwhile scientific discovery could have been made.

In another tribute, Mark Twain had commented that the 'most valuable and most constructive materials in the history of man are treasured up in India only'.

The Hindu civilisation – spanning over four millennia since the Harappan times – has had the bedrock of tolerance and pluralism all the while.

The Buddha (the Enlightened One) appeared in the sixth century BC and his teachings to alleviate human sufferings led to his wide acceptance through the subsequent millennium and half, till the eventual absorption of the Buddha as an incarnation of Vishnu. Jainism appeared around the same time holding its principle credo as non-violence, with Jain householders and monks living alongside the Hindus ever since. Sikhism was the last indigenous religion appearing in the middle of the second millennium and its holy text sings the praise of many Hindu gods.

Among the non-Indian religions, India is perhaps the only major country in the world without the taint of anti-Semitism and Indian Jews have lived for two millennia with absolute religious freedom. Christianity, too, came early. Christian communities in Kerala as followers of St. Thomas the Apostle dates back to AD 54.

There is also evidence that St. Thomas, the Canaanite, led Syrian refugees to India sometime later and achieved substantial assimilation. Islam came towards late first millennium and, with initial bloodletting battles and conquests and later with its proselytising zeal, had a very large number of converts living alongside Hindus for centuries. Mutual coexistence in the countryside is perhaps the loftiest message that Hinduism carries for other religions to this day.

Apart from religious forbearance, the Hindu civilisation has shown other signs of remarkable self-restraint. India never invaded any country in its last five millennia of history and did not attempt to become a great maritime power, although it is surrounded by oceans on three sides. The art of navigation was born in the Sindhu River 6,000 years ago. The very word 'navigation' is derived from the Sanskrit word: *nav gatih* and the word 'navy' coming from the Sanskrit *nou* (boat). Tamralipta in the east coast received Greek ships in Mauryan times. The Gupta period had many cargo ships roaming around the seacoasts and crossing the 'seven seas'. The Chola emperors had sent emissaries and priests to South Asian countries. There were guides to predict the behaviour of waters and training manuals for journeys by sea. In the North, the girdling Himalayas were not conquered by mountaineers, but were crossed over – through many difficult passes – by enlightened Buddhist monks with messages of peace and knowledge to distant China, Korea and Japan. In 500 BC, Panini described the northern highway of Asia: running from the Caspian Sea to China, as extended to Pataliputra and Tamralipta.

The land route from India to China – through Myanmar and Thailand – had become a road for common use. This road ended in Champa (central Vietnam). As early as the second century BC, the Chinese merchants travelled across northern India by this route to reach Afghanistan and Iran. Kia Tan, the Chinese writer, had referred to twenty Chinese Buddhist monks who came to India by this route in the second century AD and in whose honour the Magadha king Shrigupta built a temple.

Surely, the earlier Indian migrants had cleared and developed this road by the fourth century BC; otherwise, no common traveller would have dared to tread on this vast, unexplored expanse of all-mountainous tract. Kautilya's *Haimavata Path* was its segment and the Mahabharata described it as trans-Indus (*Pare-Sindhu*). The southern route led

Naga Sadhu, oblivious of material comforts.

from Ujjain to Paithan, leading up to Kanchipuram and Madurai.

Obviously, this was a different kind of civilisation, which did not look forward to taming Nature or subduing the environment. To the ancient *Samkhya* philosophy, Nature *(prakriti)* was organically a consort of the formless God *(purusha)*, both of whom met to make creation possible: with every object in heaven and earth being an object of worship and eulogised through great poetry. In this vast creation: Truth is one, but the Wise call it Many *(Ekam Sat, Vipra Bahudha Vadanti)*.

The fountainhead of this culture lay elsewhere: in its civilising arts and aesthetics, its elegant philosophical systems and excellent literature, its social and psychic bonds. But, behind it all, lay its holistic emphasis on science and mathematics, education and economics, sociology and logic. Six sciences were referred to in Sanskrit annals: teaching; sages in daily life including geometry; grammar; etymology; prosody and astronomy. Manu, Samkara and others preached the ethical laws. Vatsyayana laid down the science of eugenics and sex.

In Kautilya's celebrated treatise *Arthashastra* on economics, four acquisitions were described: Trinity performing *dharma;* analysis, perception and research; dialogue and communication; and the morality of punishment and retribution. A brief summary of a few ancient achievements is given below.

Formal Science

- Bhaskaracharya's (twelfth century AD) great work in mathematics *Siddhanta Shiromoni* was very popular, with *Lilavati* and *Beeja Ganita* covering arithmetic, geometry and algebra. Even trigonometry and calculus had their roots in India.

- Bhaskaracharya calculated the time taken by the earth to orbit the sun, some centuries before the Western astronomer Smart. Time taken by earth to orbit the sun had the surprising accuracy of 365.258756484 days.

- A detailed study of 'zero', the Hindu culture's seminal contribution to mathematics, is found in this work, with iterative methods of equation-solving, using unknown quantity-symbols. This included even quadratic equations, as solved by Sridharacharya (eleventh century AD).

- Reference to 'zero' *(shunya)* goes back to the Vedas and Upanishads, with mention of the decimal. The largest numbers that the Greeks and Romans used were 10–6 (10 to the power of 6), whereas the Hindus used numbers as big as 10–53 (10 to the power of 53): with specific names, during the Vedic period. Even today, the largest used number is 'Tera': 10–12 (10 to the power of 12), just getting crossed to 10–18 (10 to the power of 18).

- The standard value of 'pi' was first calculated by Bodhayana (sixth century AD), who explained the concept known as Pythagorean theorem, long before the European mathematicians. The value of 'pi' as 22/7 was confirmed in Aryabhatta II's (tenth century AD) work *Maha Siddhanta*.

Space Science

- In astronomy, the ancient Indians calculated the sizes of the sun and moon; their distances from

Dalai Lama, spreading the message of love and peace.

199

Sushruta, the father of surgery.

Material for herbal medicine.

earth; eclipse; and parallax with astronomical instruments like the water-clock and others.

- In the *Surya Siddhanta*, time measurement, sine and cosine functions, meridians, equinoxes, solstices and planetary motions (with rising and setting of Mars) were mentioned.
- The first millennium was known for its galaxy of astronomers like Varahamihir and Khana (both sixth century AD).

Medical Science

- In medicine, the treatise on life (Ayurveda) visualised clinical diagnosis and comprehensive therapy of all diseases. Dhanwantari (sixth

century BC), is believed to be the propounder of Ayurveda, whose name has become synonymous for precise diagnosis.

- Charaka (second century BC), regarded as the father of medicine, consolidated the classic encylopaedia *Charaka Samhita,* by revising the earlier medical compendium by Agnivesha. This treatise on medicine has remained a standard work over two millennia, describing anatomy, physiology, embryology, diagnosis and prognosis, and even selection and initiation of medical students and the medical oath and has been translated into Arabic and Latin in medieval times.

- Sushruta (sixth century BC) regarded as the father of surgery, was a disciple of Dhanwantari. Along with health scientists of his time, he conducted complicated surgeries like Caesareans, cataracts, artificial limbs, fractures, urinary stones, and even plastic surgery and brain surgery.
- Usage of anaesthesia was well known in ancient India. Over 125 surgical instruments were used.

Knowledge of anatomy, physiology, aetiology, embryology, digestion, metabolism, genetics and immunity is also found in many texts.

Education

- The world's first university was established in Taxila (seventh century BC), now in Pakistan. More than 10,500 students, from all over the world, studied there over 60 subjects.
- Nalanda University (fourth century BC), in Bihar, was one of the greatest institutions of ancient India in the field of education. A very

Remains of an ancient university. Scholars from all over the world flocked to the ancient universities of India, which were highly revered as seats of learning.

Mahatma Gandhi, revolutionised Hindu thought by emphasising the principles of non-violence.

Rabindranath Tagore, upheld Hindu wisdom through his writings.

large number of students, including Chinese monks and travellers, studied there the ancient scriptures, among other subjects.

• Sanskrit, as a highly developed language, was the basis of all education, with a great deal of etymology common with the European languages. According to the *Forbes* magazine (July 1987), its grammatical rigour and precision are regarded as uniquely suitable for computer software.

• In ancient education system, equal emphasis was placed on the physical, intellectual and moral aspects. Oral instructions were quite common and there were other great universities at Kashi, Valabhi and Vikramshila, besides the two mentioned above.

• Eight ways of learning derived from the gurus were: serving the teacher *(shushrusha)*, listening *(shravana)*, receiving instructions *(grahana)*, retaining *(dharana)*, discussion and debate *(uhapoha)*, seeking specialised knowledge *(vignana)*, and proving the knowledge *(tatva abhinivesha)*. Education was aimed at building the whole man with character.

Hinduism's contribution to science and civilisation has been a continuing process. It did not cease with the ancient times or in the medieval period. In the nineteenth and twentieth centuries, many Hindu thinkers of India like Raja Ram Mohan Roy, Ramakrishna Paramhamsa, Swami Vivekananda, Rabindranath Tagore and Sri Aurobindo in the East; Mahatma Gandhi, Bal Gangadhar Tilak and Swami Dayanand in the West; Ramana Maharshi, C. Rajagopalachari, J. Krishnamurty and S. Radhakrishnan in the South; and Jawaharlal

Nehru in the North have all contributed to the philosophical and social bedrock of Indian thought. Many contemporary scientists like J.C. Bose, P.C. Ray, C.V. Raman, Meghnad Saha, S.N. Bose, Birbal Sahni, P.C. Mahalanobis, Homi Bhava, Vikram Sarabhai, S. Chandrasekhar and Hargovind Khorana had also contributed to scientific research.

Those who had enriched the field of fine arts and performing arts have been a legion. For the USA alone, a virtual 'diaspora dictionary' has been compiled as follows:

- **The Digerati** – Nearly 500,000 high-technology professionals work and contribute in industry and academia, business and finance. They have burnished the Indian reputation as 'smart' engineers and entrepreneurs: as the 'new icons' in HP, Pepsi, Motorola and Berkshire Hathway.
- **The Illuminati** – These are the thinkers, teachers, writers and researchers. From Amartya Sen in economics to C.K. Prahalad in business, they are leaders in thought. They are now proliferating in 'think-tanks' like the Carnegie Endowment and Newsweek International.
- **The Literati and the Glitterati:** India's 'soft power' has never been more evident. Indian-American writers continue to make waves, with new names like Jhumpa Lahiri and Suketu Mehta leaving indelible marks in literature. Similarly, Deepa Mehta and Gurinder Kaur are making successful inroads into movies.
- **The Drudgerati:** They drive cabs, run gas stations, manage newsstands and own liquor stores. At the higher end, they own 20,000 of America's 53,000 budget- and mid-priced franchises:

worth \$37 billion. Indians also own the nation's 134,000 convenience stores: worth \$80 billion.

The key to the twenty-first century lies not only in the Indian resilience and the synergetic nature of its all-absorbing liberal, cultural values, but also in the fact that ancient India never looked at human beings in parts: as body or mind or soul, but as an integrated whole, a complete Man, a miniature Divinity, a spark of the Great Fire, a ray of the Eternal Light.

In this recognition lies the seed of renaissance: where every science and civilising art in the Hindu way of life is never an isolated phenomenon, but closely related to the general mien of acquiring knowledge and conducting collective welfare for all mankind – embedded in the highest traditions of tolerance and peace for other faiths, so needed by the world of the twenty-first century. India continues its search for meaning and relevance in a world that is increasingly complex. It can always draw from more than three millennia of recorded science and philosophy and a resilience of spirit that few other regions of the world are heir to.

It is the Hindu celebration of life that is seen in so many forms and manifestations: blended, assimilated and absorbed, culminating in a way of life that is unique as well as special. This is the joy of life that is saluted the world over.

Further Reading

Abbot, J. *Indian Ritual and Belief: The Keys of Power*. New Delhi: Usha, 1984.

Bahadur Singh, I.J. *Indians in Southeast Asia*. New Delhi: Sterling Publications, 1982.

———. *Indians in Caribbean*. New Delhi: Sterling Publications, 1987.

Basu, Nandalal. *DristiíOí Shristi* (Bengali). Calcutta: Viswa Bharati, 1986.

Bharata. *The Natya Shastra*. Translated by a board of scholars. New Delhi: Sri Satguru Publications, 1992.

Bradnock, Robert and Rana, eds. *1996 India Handbook*. Bath: Trade & Travel Handbook, 1995.

Chatterjee, Satishchandra and Dutta Dhirendramohan. *An Introduction to Indian Philosophy*. Calcutta: University of Calcutta, 1960.

Chattopadhyay, Kamaladevi. *Handicrafts of India*. Delhi: Indian Council for Cultural Relations, 1985.

Devi, Pria and Richard Kavin. *ADITI—A Celebration of Life*. New Delhi: Motilal Banarasidas, 1987.

Frauwallner Erich. *History of Indian Philosophy*. Translated by V.M. Bedekar. Delhi: Motilal Banarasidas, 1984.

Ghosh, Vidya, ed. *Tirth: The Treasury of Indian Expressions*. New Delhi: CMC Ltd, 1992.

Gopal Sastri, S.N. *Elements of Indian Aesthetics*. Varanasi: Chaukhamba Orientalia, 1983.

Gopal, Surendra. *Indians in Russia*. New Delhi: ICHR, 1988.

Gupta, Shakti M. *Festivals, Fairs and Fasts of India*. Delhi: Clarion Books, 1990.

Gupta, Shyamala. *Art, Beauty and Creativity: Indian and Western Aesthetics*. New Delhi: D.K. Printworld, 1999.

Hillebrandt, Alfred. *Vedic Mythology*. Translated by Sreeramula Rajeswara Sarma. Delhi: Motilal Banarasidas, 1996.

Hiriyanna, M. *Art Experience*. Mysore: Kavyalaya Publications, 1954.

Judge, Paramjit S. *Punjabis in Canada*. New Delhi: Chalukya Publications, 1994.

Kanchan, R.K. *Hindu Kingdoms of Southeast Asia*. New Delhi: Cosmos Publications, 1990.

Kaplan, Abraham. *The New World of Philosophy*. New York: Vintage Book, 1961.

Karve, Iraavati. *Hindu Society—An Introduction*. Bombay: Deshmukh Prakasan, 1961.

Kundu, Arunesh. 'Hindu Dharma Ki O Kanoî' (Bengali). *Sananda*, May 20, 2000.

Machwe, Prabhakar. *Hinduism—Its Contribution to Science and Civilisation*. New Delhi: Vikas Publications, 1979.

Maxwell, T.S. *The Gods of Asia: Image, Text and Meaning*. New Delhi: Oxford University Press, 1977.

Modi, Dr Bhupendra K. *Hinduism: the Universal Truth*. New Delhi: Brijbasi, 1993.

Mookherjee, Ajit. *Kundalini: The Arousal of the Inner Energy*. New Delhi: Clarion Books, 1982.

———. *Ritual Art of India*. London: Thames & Hudson, 1985.

Panikkar, K.M. *Hindu Society at Cross-roads*. Bombay: Asia Publishing House, 1961.

Parimoo, Ratan and Indramohan Sharma. *Creative Arts in Modern India: Essays in Comparative Criticism*. Vols. 1 and 2. New Delhi: Books & Books, 1995.

Parminder, Geoffrey. *Asian Religions*. New Delhi: Sterling Publications, 1977.

Radhakrishnan, Sarvepalli. *Indian Philosophies*. Vols. 1 and 2. New York: Macmillan, 1958.

Radhakrishnan, Sarvepalli and Charles A. Moore. *A Source Book in Indian Philosophy*. New Jersey: Princeton, 1960.

Ramanujam, A.K. *Folktales from India*. New Delhi: Viking, 1993.

Reddy, E.S., ed. *Indian South Africans*. New Delhi: Sanchar Publications, 1993.

Sahadevan, P. *India and Overseas Indians*. New Delhi: Kalinga Publications, 1995.

Seidenberg, Dana April. *Uhniu and the Kenya Indians*. New Delhi: Vikas Publications, 1983.

Sivaramamurti, C. *South Indian Paintings*. New Delhi: Publications Division, 1994.

Smith, Huston. *The World's Religions*. New Delhi: Harper Collins Publications, 1997.

Stutley, Margaret. *Ancient Indian Magic and Folklore*. Delhi: Motilal Banarasidas, 1980.

Suda, J. P. *Religions in India*. New Delhi: Sterling Publications, 1978.

Sudhi, Padma. *Aesthetic Theories of India*. Vol. 1. Pune: Bhandarkar Oriental Res. Instt., 1983.

Tagore, Abanindranath. *Bageshwari Shilpa Prabandhabali* (Bengali). Calcutta: Rupa, 1963.

Tawney, C.H. *The Katha Sarit Sagar: Or Ocean of the Streams of Story*. Vols. 1 and 2. Delhi: Munshiram Manoharlal, 1968.

Thomas, P. *Hindu Religion, Custom and Manners*. Mumbai: D.B. Taraporavala, 1975.

Vatsyayan, Kapila. *The Square and the Circle of Indian Arts*. New Delhi: Roli Books, 1983.

Verma, Rajendra. *The World of Vedic Life and Culture: The Vedas and Cosmic Poetry*. Delhi: Sharada Prakashan, 1990.

Wood, Anand. *From the Upanishads*. New Delhi: Full Circle, 1997.

Zimmer, Heinrich and Campbell Joseph, ed. *Philosophies of India*. New York: Princeton University Press, 1969.

http://www.atributetohinduism.com

http://www.yogapoint.com

http://www.iskcon.org.uk

http://www.hindunet.org

Index

Photo Credits

DN Chaudhury : 43, 49, 59, 60, 64 (both), 65, 67.

India Picture cover I – 1, 7, 9, 12, 16, 22-23, 25, 26-27, 37, 40-41, 44-45, 48, 51, 53, 54, 56-57, 58, 61, 65, 71, 72, 73, 74-75, 76-77, 85, 89, 100, 103, 106, 118, 126, 130-131, 134, 140 (R), 142-143, 146-147, 149, 151, 153, 154, 158-159, 164, 165, 166, 167, 171, 172, 176-177, 178, 180, 182-183, 194-195, 198, 199.

Prakash Israni – 11, 18, 20, 28, 35, 36, 42, 52, 68, 81, 128-129, 198.

Wild Photos – 14-15, 46-47, 63, 66, 78, 86-87, 88, 98-99, 120, 124-125, 132-133, 135, 139, 140(L), 150, 160, 162-163, 175.